The NYCLU Guide to Women's Rights in New York State

THE NYCLU GUIDE TO Women's Rights IN NEW YORK STATE

•

EVE CARY

PANTHEON BOOKS, NEW YORK

Library of Congress Cataloging in Publication Data

Cary, Eve.
The NYCLU Guide to Women's Rights in New York State.

1. Women—Legal status, laws, etc.—New York (State) 2. Women's rights—New York (State) I. Title.
KFN5111.W6C37   342′.747′087   77-91025
ISBN 0-394-73586-2

Manufactured in the United States of America

First Edition

For my mother, Barbara Cary

Contents

Acknowledgments

The publication of this book was made possible by the assistance, advice, research and critical review of the following people, to whom NYCLU is extremely grateful:

Ellen Azorin, for concept, design and production:
Janet Benshoof, Director, Reproductive Freedom Project, ACLU;
Peter Bienstock, staff counsel, Puerto Rican Legal Defense and Education Fund;
John W. Corwin, staff attorney, Center for Constitutional Rights;
Deborah Eisenberg, NYCLU staff;
Karen Farraguna, Legal Aid attorney;
Doris Jonas Freed, attorney and author;
Ruth Bader Ginsberg, Professor, Columbia Law School;
Kristin Booth Glen, attorney;
Emily Goodman, attorney;
Beverly Gross, General Counsel, District Council 37, AFSCME;
Florine Israel, NYCLU staff;
Sylvia Law, Professor, New York University Law School;
Alan Levine, staff counsel, NYCLU;
William Liebovitz, attorney;
Cookie Lipschultz, law student;
Bernice Malamud, insurance consultant;
Sally McGee, Coordinator, Anti-Rape Committee, Manhattan Women's Political Caucus;
Michael O'Connor, Welfare Coordinator, Community Action For Legal Services;
Kathleen Peratis, Director, ACLU Women's Rights Project;
Diane Schulder, attorney;
Ronni Smith, Director, Management Services, New York State Division of Human Rights;

Special thanks must go to NYCLU's Associate Director, Barbara Shack, who was the moving spirit behind this publication, and to Ann Barcher, a voluntary attorney who contributed a great deal to the research and writing.

—Eve Cary

The NYCLU Guide
to
Women's Rights
in New York State

1. INTRODUCTION

Virtually all of the law in the area of women's rights has developed in the past decade. During this period, both federal and state courts have decided women's rights cases and the various legislatures have enacted women's rights laws. To add to the confusion, some of these laws duplicate each other while others conflict. The result is that few women are really sure what rights they have in any particular situation.

The purpose of this book is to present as complete a picture as possible of women's rights as they exist in New York State—under both state and federal law—and to identify the source of these rights (whether a court case or a statute, a state law or a federal law).* In addition, the book describes how a woman can go about getting rights she has been denied. Sometimes simply knowing your rights and being able to point to the law that insures them may be enough to get what you're entitled to. An employer or rental agent or school official may change a discriminatory policy simply upon having it pointed out by someone who knows what she's talking about. More often, however, women will have to file complaints with human rights agencies or in court to challenge discrimination. This book is intended only to get you started in the right direction. *It is not a substitute for a lawyer.* Laws are changing daily and each case in the end wins or loses on its individual facts. A good lawyer is essential in most cases to make sure that your case is presented properly.

Women are, of course, affected by all of our laws. This book, however, is devoted only to those laws that affect them specifically as women. Some areas of law are omitted because, although they have a disproportionate effect on women, they are better discussed in a different context. For example, prostitution is not covered because, although virtually only women are charged with the crime, once arrested, their cases are handled similarly to any other criminal charge, and the rights of an alleged prostitute are the same as those of any other criminal

---

*Citations are noted in brackets following the rights to which they refer.

defendant.** The aspects of prostitution laws that particularly discriminate against women are sociological rather than legal and thus are beyond the scope of this book. A discussion of the laws affecting lesbians is also omitted (except for a brief mention of child custody cases), because there are virtually no laws protecting gay people.***

Many of the laws discussed in this book prohibit not only sex discrimination, but also discrimination based on race, religion, ethnic background, age and disability. If you need more information about these other types of discrimination, call the agencies referred to in the section on Procedures.

If you don't know your rights, you obviously can't stand up for them. No matter what legislatures, courts and lawyers do, women will remain the victims of rampant discrimination until they know their rights and demand them. This book, then, should tell you what you have a legal right to demand and how to go about it.

A Note On Citation

You will see that following the names of cited cases are a series of numbers and letters. The numbers refer to the volume and page of the volume in which the case is printed. If the letters "U.S." appear in the citation, the case was decided by the United States Supreme Court. "F." refers to a Federal court case and "N.Y." to a New York State court case. Other citations are to statutes and administrative agency regulations.

2. PROCEDURES:
How to go about making the law work for you

Federal, state and New York City laws protect women against sex discrimination. Different government agencies enforce these anti-discrimination laws at the three levels. Because federal agencies are responsible for hearing federal law complaints from all over the country, you will often get faster action if you pursue your remedies under State law.

New York State law

The New York State Human Rights Law prohibits discrimination on the basis of sex and marital status in a variety of areas, including credit, employment, public accommodations and housing, and on the basis of marital status only in private, non-sectarian schools [*Exec. Law §296*]. This means, for example, that a landlord cannot refuse to rent you an apartment because you are a woman or because you are single and he thinks that you would be a less stable tenant than a married couple. Similarly, an employer cannot refuse to hire you either because you are a woman or because you are married and he thinks two incomes in one household are a luxury. The New York State Division of Human Rights enforces the State Human Rights Law (see sections on housing, credit, employment, and public accommodations) and will assign its own attorneys to present your case if it goes to a public hearing. If you think that your rights under the state law have been violated, you can also choose to bring a suit in state court, but you will have to hire your own attorney.

New York City law

If you live in any of the five boroughs of New York City, you are also protected by the New York City Human Rights Code, enforced by the City Commission on Human Rights. This law prohibits sex discrimination in employment, housing and public accommodations, and also prohibits discrimination on the basis of marital status in housing, and sale or rental of land and commercial space [*Administrative Code §B1-7.0*]..

How to file a discrimination complaint

[*The procedures described below refer to State complaints; New York City procedures are parallel, with the few exceptions listed under "New York City Commission on Human Rights."*]

You can file a discrimination complaint in person or by mail. Call the main office of the State Division at (212) 488-5750 and ask them for the address and telephone number of your regional office. If you are unable to file a complaint in person, explain the details over the telephone and ask that a complaint be prepared and mailed to you for your review and notarized signature.

Time limitations

The complaint must be filed within one year after the discrimination occurred or you will lose your right to file.

Complaint

The complaint should contain the following information:
1. A list of names, titles, business addresses and telephone numbers of those you think acted unlawfully;
2. A summary of the discriminatory acts complained of (include dates if possible);
3. A list of the details of any financial loss you suffered due to discrimination (salary difference between male and female employees, for instance).

Finding of no probable cause

Once your complaint has been received, the office will investigate the charge and decide if there is "probable cause" to believe your complaint is valid. If no probable cause is found, your complaint will be dismissed, at which point you have 15 days to appeal the decision to the Human Rights Appeal Board, which is separate from the Division. If you want a lawyer on appeal, you must get your own. On appeal, the Board may agree that the case should be dismissed or it may instruct the Division to reopen the case. If dismissed, you can appeal the Board's decision to the Appellate Division of the State Supreme Court. You will need your own lawyer to represent you on appeal to the court. If you win and your opponent appeals, the Division lawyer will continue to represent the case in favor of your complaint.

Finding of probable cause

If the Division finds there is probable cause to support your complaint, it will try to get you and the party charged with having discriminated (respondent) to come to an agreement (conciliation) which will accord you your rights and eliminate any unlawful discrimination. If an agreement cannot be reached, the complaint will be scheduled for a public hearing, similar to a trial, at which a Division attorney will be assigned to present your case to a hearing officer at the Division. You may wish to retain your own attorney to represent your interests during the conciliation proceedings and/or the hearing. If you choose to do this, at the hearing you can have the case in support of your complaint presented by your attorney alone or by your attorney and the Division attorney.

After the hearing, a decision is recommended by the hearing examiner and an order is issued by the State Commissioner of Human Rights. If discrimination is found, the party charged will be ordered to stop the discriminatory practices and to take action to cure the results of past discrimination (e.g., pay you back wages). An investigation will be conducted, usually within one year, to make sure the order is carried out. If your opponent appeals the Commissioner's decision, the Division lawyer will continue to present the case in favor of your complaint.

If the hearing officer dismisses the complaint, finding no discrimination, you have 15 days from the date of the order to appeal the decision to the Human Rights Appeal Board. If you wish to be represented by a lawyer on this appeal, you will have to get your own. The State Division will not represent you on an appeal from its dismissal of your complaint. At the appeal, your case can be orally argued or presented as a written argument. If you are not satisfied with the Appeal Board's decision you have the right to appeal to the Appellate Division of the State Supreme Court.

Retaliation

The Human Rights Law specifically protects you against retaliation by your employer if you file a discrimination complaint. You should file a complaint of retaliation if your employer punished you in some way (e.g., discharge, demotion, different assignment of duties) solely because you made a complaint [*Exec. Law §296 (1)(e)*].

If a group of women has been affected by discrimination in a similar manner, it is possible to make a group complaint or a "class action." If successful, this action would provide relief for all women in the class. If you think you might want to file a class action, you should consult an attorney.

New York City Commission on Human Rights

The procedure for filing a complaint with the New York City Commission on Human Rights for violations of the New York City Human Rights Code is the same as the State Division's procedure except for the following points:

1. You have 30 days to ask the Chair of the Commission in writing for a review of a decision dismissing your complaint if the Commission decides there is no probable cause to continue the investigation;
2. If the Commission's final decision after the hearing is unfavorable to you, you have 30 days to ask for a review of the decision by the Appellate Division of the New York Supreme Court. At this stage you will need your own lawyer.

Federal remedies

If you have a complaint about sex discrimination in employment, you are probably protected by Title VII of the 1964 Civil Rights Act which is enforced by the Equal Employment Opportunity Commission (EEOC). You must file your Title VII complaint within 300 days of the discriminatory act. (See Section on Employment.) You may pursue your Title VII remedy exclusively or you may file a complaint simultaneously with the State or City human rights agency. If you file your complaint directly with the State Divison of Human Rights, you may ask the Division to file your complaint also with the EEOC or you may do it yourself no later than 300 days after the incident occurred or 30 days after receiving notice that the Division has completed its action, whichever is earlier. You can then pursue Title VII relief if you are dissatisfied with the Division's action. If you file only with the EEOC, that agency will give the State Division your case to work on for at least 60 days and then may take it back if you are not satisfied with the State's action or if the State does not act within that time. Because of the tremendous backlog of cases at the EEOC and the broader protections of the State Human Rights Law, filing with the State Division will usually bring the quickest results. To protect yourself on all fronts and minimize delay, you should file in both places at the same time.

The procedure at the EEOC is similar to that at the Division: You file your complaint; an investigation will be conducted, and either a finding of probable cause made or the complaint dismissed. If there is a finding of probable cause, conciliation proceedings between you and your employer will be attempted. If no agreement can be reached, the EEOC may agree to bring a lawsuit in federal court on your behalf or it will issue you a "Right to Sue" letter and you can hire a lawyer and bring it yourself. If the EEOC dismisses the complaint, it will automatically issue the letter so that you can go to court if you choose to. The EEOC has exclusive jurisdiction over complaints of employment discrimination under Title VII, which means that you must file your complaint with them. You may not go to a federal court until the EEOC has had the opportunity to act on your complaint. After the EEOC has had the complaint for 180 days, however, whether or not it has acted on it, you may request it to issue you a Right to Sue letter and you can then proceed directly into federal court with your own attorney. You have 90 days after receiving a Right to Sue letter to go to court.

Addresses

Following are the addresses and telephone numbers of the offices of the various human rights agencies.

1. Equal Employment Opportunity Commission

Federal Plaza
New York, N.Y. 10007
212) 264-7161
(If you live outside New York City, you will be referred to your local office.)

2. State of New York Division of Human Rights

Administrative Office:
Two World Trade Center
New York, N.Y. 10047
(212) 488-5750

Complaints should be made to one of the regional offices:

ALBANY 12210
217 Lark Street
(518) 474-2705

BINGHAMTON 13901
44 Hawley Street
(607) 773-7713

BRONX 10459
1029 East 163rd Street
(212) 328-6900

BROOKLYN 11201
16 Court Street
(212) 852-0313

BUFFALO 14202
69 Delaware Avenue
(716) 842-4456

HAUPPAUGE (Suffolk Co.) 11787
State Office Building
Veterans Highway
(516) 979-5005

HEMPSTEAD (Nassau Co.) 11550
183 Fulton Avenue
(516) 538-1360

MANHATTAN (Lower) 10007
270 Broadway (9th floor)
(212) 488-5384

MANHATTAN (Upper) 10027
163 West 125th Street
(212) 678-2303

QUEENS 11435
89-14 Sutphin Boulevard
(212) 291-6646

ROCHESTER 14614
65 Broad Street
(716) 325-2367

SYRACUSE 13202
100 New Street
(315) 473-8215

WHITE PLAINS 10603
30 Glenn Street
(914) 949-4394

3. State of New York Human Rights Appeal Board

Two World Trade Center
New York, N.Y. 10047

4. New York City Commission on Human Rights

52 Duane Street
New York, N.Y. 10007
(212) 566-5050

3. EMPLOYMENT

The law

Federal, state and local laws require employers to treat women and men identically with respect to all aspects of employment including hiring, promotion, wages and job benefits (e.g. seniority rights, insurance coverage and benefits, pensions and vacation time and pay). New York state law also prohibits employment discrimination based on marital status. This means that an employer cannot, for example, refuse to hire a married woman because he thinks that family responsibilities might interfere with her work.

All of the following practices are prohibited under federal, state and New York City law [*42 U.S.C. 2000e et seq. as amended by the EEO Act of 1972; N.Y. Executive Law §296; N.Y.C. Admin. Code Chapter 1 Title B §B1-7.0*].

1) An employer may not:
- hire, fire or provide different salaries or benefits to employees based on sex;
- refuse to allow a job applicant of one sex to file an application for employment while accepting an application from a person of the opposite sex;
- pass over for promotion a qualified employee on the basis of sex.

2) Neither employers nor employment agencies may advertise job openings for one sex only (e.g. "young man wanted . . .")

3) An employment agency may not:
- refuse to refer any person's job application to an employer because of the applicant's sex;
- refuse to hire an applicant for one of its job listings on the basis of sex;
- classify applicants and job listings by sex.

4) A labor organization may not exclude or expel from membership, refuse to refer for employment, or cause or try to cause an employer to discriminate against any person on the basis of sex. (A union will not be violating the law simply because it asks applicants to state their sex on a membership ap-

plication, but if it engages in other discriminatory practices, the State Division of Human Rights will take note of the fact that the question is routinely asked and may question the motive for it.)

5) An employer, labor organization or employment agency may not deny admission into apprenticeship or training programs to any person on the basis of sex; or advertise those programs in such a way as to discourage persons of one sex from applying.

6) An employer, labor organization or employment agency may not retaliate against any person through threats, discharge, demotion etc. because she or he filed a complaint of an unlawful employment practice.

Bona fide occupational qualifications

There is only one situation in which an employer may lawfully use sex as a hiring criterion. This is when he can prove that sex is a bona fide occupational qualification (BFOQ). [*EEOC Guidelines on Discrimination Because of Sex, 29 C.F.R. §1604.2 (1972)*]. For example, an employer may lawfully hire only women for the job of ladies' room attendant, or only male actors to play male roles in the theater.

There are very few jobs for which sex is a BFOQ, however, and you should examine the duties of any job carefully before accepting an employer's claim. For example, many airlines have argued that sex is a BFOQ for the job of stewardess, but the courts have consistently held that there is nothing inherent in the job that requires the person performing it to be female. [*Diaz v. Pan American World Airways, Inc. 442 F. 2d 385 (5th Cir. 1971)*].

Stereotypes as hiring criteria

Employers are prohibited from limiting jobs to persons of one sex on the basis of stereotypes concerning the abilities of *most* women or *most* men. For example, although it may be true that most women are not as strong as most men, and, therefore, jobs requiring heavy manual labor will generally be performed by men, an employer may not refuse to hire the exceptional woman who is strong enough to perform a heavy job simply because the majority of women would be incapable of handling it. An employer must give you a chance to try out for a job. The fact that it may be easier for an employer to limit certain jobs to men only is not a lawful reason for refusing a woman's job application. [*Bowe v. Colgate-Palmolive Co., 416 F.2d 711 (7th Cir. 1969)*].

Job-related tests

An employer may not give pre-employment tests to job applicants (including minimum height and weight measurements) that have the effect of excluding more women than men unless he or she can prove that the test is "job-related." To be job-related a test must actually measure the skills required to perform the job *[Dothard v. Rawlinson,—U.S.—,53 L. Ed. 2d 786 (1977)*; Sontag v. Bronstein 33 N.Y. 2d 197 (1973)*]. Thus, while it might be lawful to require applicants for the job of construction worker to lift a heavy weight as part of a pre-employment test, it would not be lawful to require persons applying for the job of English professor to pass a weight-lifting test.

"Sex Plus"

Courts have held that an employer who discriminates against only particular groups of women is still violating the law. For example, an employer may not refuse to hire mothers, but not fathers, of young children. Even though he may hire many unmarried or childless women, he is still guilty of sex discrimination, if he makes sex-plus-something-else, such as motherhood, a basis for refusing to hire or fire [*Phillips v. Martin-Marietta, 400 U.S. 542 (1971)*].*

Pregnancy

Various court and agency decisions have established a number of rights for pregnant women.

The general rule is that pregnant women must be treated like everyone else for purposes of employment. If a woman is not disabled by pregnancy, she must be treated like all other healthy employees. When she becomes disabled, she must be treated just like other disabled employees.

This section will explain how New York law provides better protection for pregnant workers than federal law in certain ways. Some rights of pregnant women *under federal law* may change because these issues are before Congress and the U.S.

---

*Reproduced in appendix to Chapter 3.

Supreme Court as we go to press. If you have a problem involving pregnancy discrimination in employment you will probably do better filing your complaint with the appropriate New York State agency. If you are not sure how to proceed, consult a lawyer.

1) Hiring and Firing: It is unlawful for an employer to fire or refuse to hire a pregnant woman who is capable of performing her job, and for an employment agency to refuse to refer a pregnant woman for employment.

2) Maternity Leave: It is unlawful for an employer to have a blanket rule requiring pregnant employees to take a mandatory maternity leave at some arbitrary point in their pregnancy, e.g., five months. Each woman's case must be dealt with on an individual basis and a woman must be permitted to continue working as long as she is capable of performing her job. The fact that a woman deals with the public in the course of her job is not a reason for forcing her on maternity leave [*Cleveland Board of Education v. LaFleur, 414 U.S. 632 (1974),* * *Union Free School Dist. v. New York State etc. 35 N.Y. 2d 371 (1974)*].

3) Sick leave: Under state (but not federal) law, disability caused by pregnancy must be treated the same as any other short-term disability. That is, if an employer provides paid sick leave to his employees, he must permit a woman to use her sick leave when she is disabled by pregnancy or childbirth. Similarly, an employer who permits employees to take leaves of absence for other reasons must permit a woman to use her leave of absence as maternity leave. [*Board of Education of Union Free School Dist. No. 2 v. N.Y. State Div. of Human Rights 35 NY 2d 673 (1974); Board of Education of the City of New York v. State Division of Human Rights 35 N.Y. 2d 675 (1974); Board of Education of Union Free School District No. 22 v. New York State Division of Human Rights 35 N.Y. 2d 677 (1974)*].

4) Disability insurance benefits: Under New York law (but not federal law) pregnant workers are entitled to disability insurance benefits to replace lost wages if they are disabled and unable to work because of pregnancy or childbirth. Private employees are covered by different laws than government employees.

　　a) *Private employees* are covered by the New York State Disability Benefits Law (DBL), Article 9 of the Workmen's

---

*Reproduced in appendix to Chapter 3.

Compensation Law, enforced by the Disability Benefits Bureau of the Workmen's Compensation Board. This requires all private employers to provide all employees disability insurance benefits for up to 26 weeks if they become totally disabled and unable to work. Originally, this law did not cover pregnancy-related disabilities. However, in August, 1977, this law was amended to include disabilities that arise in connection with pregnancy or childbirth. Now under the DBL law a woman may receive up to 8 weeks of disability benefits for a normal childbirth and up to 26 weeks of benefits if there are complications of the pregnancy or childbirth [*L. 1977, Ch. 675 §§1, 28, 29, 86*].

If you become disabled because of pregnancy or childbirth, file a claim for benefits with your employer or with the employer's insurance company. Use the official (DBL) form and keep a copy for yourself, making a note of the date you filed it. You may obtain a DBL form from your employer or from: Workmen's Compensation Board, Disability Benefits Bureau, Two World Trade Center, Room 3790, New York, N.Y. 10047.

If you receive a rejection notice, it will come in three copies. Use the reverse side to request a review. Send two of the copies to the Workmen's Compensation Board and keep one.

If you do not receive the benefits *or* get a rejection, write directly to the DBL Bureau, 1949 North Broadway, Albany, N.Y. 12201 and ask that the claim be investigated.

If your disability occurred before August 3, 1977, you may still request disability benefits from your employer as long as you do so within a year of the disability period. You are entitled to disability benefits because even prior to the new DBL law, the New York State Human Rights Law required that disability coverage provided by employers must cover pregnancy-related disabilities [*Brooklyn Union Gas Company v. New York State Division of Human Rights 41 N.Y. 2d 84 (1977)*]. If your employer will not provide benefits for disabilities that occurred before August 1977, you should file a complaint with the State Division of Human Rights.

b) *Government employees* are *not* covered by the DBL law described above, but *are* covered by State Human Rights Law which requires all disability plans to cover pregnancy-related disabilities [*Brooklyn Union Gas Company, supra*]. If you are covered by a disability plan, you are then entitled to pregnancy disability benefits. If your disability claim is rejected, you should file a complaint with the State Division of Human Rights.

Whether you are a government or private employee you are entitled to the same benefits for pregnancy-related disabilities as your employer provides for all other disabilities (e.g., heart attacks or broken legs). The law in this area is still not entirely settled. In spite of the limitations contained in the new DBL on payments for pregnancy-related disabilities, it is possible that, if you are receiving lower payments or shorter periods of coverage for pregnancy disability, you may have a sex discrimination complaint. If you need more information to determine whether you are being discriminated against, call the State Division of Human Rights or the New York Civil Liberties Union.

5) Unemployment Insurance: A pregnant woman capable of working may not be denied unemployment compensation if she is otherwise entitled to it, nor may the state impose more stringent requirements on her than on other people in order to get it (e.g., making her apply for 15 jobs per week when other people need apply for only 5) [*Turner v. Department of Employment Security 423 U.S. 44 (1975)*].

Keep in mind that you are entitled to have pregnancy and childbirth treated like other disabilities only when you are actually disabled. Employers are not required to give pregnant employees child-rearing leave. If you voluntarily leave your job to prepare for the birth of your child before you are actually physically disabled, or if you decide to stay home for several months to care for your baby after you have recovered from giving birth, you forfeit the rights described above.

Who is covered by which laws
Title VII applies to:
1) Private, state and municipal employers with at least 15

employees;
2) Employment agencies;
3) Labor organizations with at least 15 members;
4) Federal-State Training and Employment Service System;
5) Joint labor-management apprenticeship programs;
6) Federal employees.(The Civil Service Commission, not the EEOC, enforces Title VII in the case of complaints by federal employees. Consult the equal opportunity counselor of your federal agency.)

State Human Rights Law applies to:
1) Private employers with at least 4 employees;
2) Employment agencies;
3) State and municipal government employees (eligibility and certification may be limited to one sex for state civil service jobs which relate to institutional custody and care of persons of the same sex);
4) Public and private educational institutions (See section on Education);
5) Federal-State Training and Employment Service System;

New York City Human Rights Law applies to:
1) Private employers with at least 4 employees;
2) Employment agencies;
3) Labor organizations;
4) Municipal employees.

Remedy

Any woman who believes she has been discriminated against in employment because of her sex should file a charge against the offending party with the Equal Employment Opportunity Commission and with the State Division of Human Rights (See Chapter 2). To make a complaint about denial of benefits for disability caused by pregnancy, you should call the State Division at (212) 488-5750.

Equal Pay Acts

Other laws that protect women against discrimination in employment are the Federal and State Equal Pay Acts which require that a woman and a man doing substantially the same work be paid at the same rate [*Equal Pay Act 29 U.S.C. 206(d), U.S. Dept. of Labor Reg. 29 CFR 800, N.Y. Labor Laws §194,*

Educ. Law §3026]. The jobs may have different titles and do not have to be identical, but if they require equal skill, effort and responsibility, the persons who perform them are entitled to equal pay, benefits, overtime and vacation pay. For example, a nurse's aide and a hospital orderly may be entitled to equal pay.

Differing rates of pay for substantially similar work are legally permissible only if the difference is based on a non-discriminatory seniority or merit system or a system that measures earning by quality or quantity of production.

These laws apply to any employer whose employees are subject to minimum wage laws.

If you believe that you are being paid less than a man doing the same work, get in contact with the Wage and Hour Division of the U.S. Dept. of Labor or the New York State Dept. of Labor. You can file a complaint with either agency, both of which will protect your identity from your employer. If the agency finds after investigation that your employer is discriminating, it will request him to comply with the law in the future and require him to give up to two years back pay to those who suffered the wage differential. If the employer refuses to comply, either you or the Department of Labor on your behalf can bring a lawsuit for the back pay as well as lawyers' fees and the other costs of going to court. If you sue on your own, you can get twice the amount you lost in back pay for two years before the date the lawsuit was filed and three if the violation was "willful."

You must bring the suit within two years after you have suffered pay discrimination. This period may be extended to three years if you can show that the company discriminated willfully. It is a good idea also to file a charge of employment discrimination with the State Division of Human Rights at the same time you file your equal pay complaint.

Government contracts

Any employer who has a contract with the federal, state or local government is prohibited from discriminating against women.

If you have a discrimination complaint against an employer who holds a government contract, it is still best to file an Equal Pay Act complaint and/or a complaint with the Human Rights Division. If the employer holds a *federal* contract you may also file a complaint with:

Director of the Office of Federal Contract Compliance
Department of Labor
Washington, D.C. 20210

For discrimination by an employer with a *state* contract, get in contact with The New York State Division of Human Rights, 2 World Trade Center, New York, N.Y. 10047. In each case you should describe the nature of the discrimination and give the name, address and telephone number of the employer.

4. EDUCATION

Students at public schools in New York are protected against sex discrimination in education by the 14th Amendment to the United States Constitution and by both state and federal statutes.

New York law

Curriculum: New York's Education Law provides that: "Notwithstanding any general, special, local law or rule or regulation of the education department to the contrary, no person shall be refused admission into or be excluded from any course of instruction offered in the state public and high school systems by reason of that person's sex." [*Education Law §3201-(a) (McKinney Supp. 1976)*]. This means that there can be no requirement that girls, but not boys, must take home economics or a rule permitting only boys and not girls to attend woodshop class.

Athletics: The law also provides that no student shall be rejected from state public and high school athletic teams because of her/his sex. [*Education Law §3201-(a) (McKinney Supp. 1976)*]. However, the State Education Commissioner is allowed to make and has made the following regulations concerning physical education *(8 NYCRR 135.4(c)(7)(ii)(c)]:*

1. In schools that do not provide separate competition for male and female students in a specific sport, no student shall be excluded from such competition solely by reason of sex, except:

2. There shall be no mixed competition in the following sports: basketball, boxing, football, ice hockey, rugby and wrestling.

3. In the sports of baseball, field hockey, lacrosse, soccer, softball, speedball, team handball and power volleyball where the height of the net is set at less than eight feet, the fitness of a given student to participate in mixed competition shall be determined by a review panel consisting of the school physician, a physical education teacher designated by the principal of the school, and if

requested by the parents of the pupil, a physician selected by such parents.

4. In schools that provide separate competition for male and female pupils in interschool athletic competition in a specific sport, the principal or the chief executive officer of the school may permit a female or females to participate on a male team in sports other than those set forth in subclause (2) of this clause. However, where separate competition is provided, males may not participate on teams organized for females.

The school board must divide its money, facilities and personnel equitably between males and females to make sure that women develop their athletic skills to the limits of their potential [*8 NYCRR 135.4(c) (f)*]. Thus, if a school provides programs for males in sports and gymnastics, there must also be comparable athletic programs for female students.

Marriage, pregnancy, and parenthood: Guidelines set out by the Commissioner of Education provide that the opportunity to participate in all the activities of the school attended may not be restricted or denied solely because a student is married, pregnant, or a parent. Pregnant women students in New York City are entitled not only to continue attending their regular school throughout the entire pregnancy, but may exercise the option to attend a full school program at a special center. A girl who leaves school while pregnant may return after the birth of her child. [*Guidelines for Students Rights and Responsibilities, State Education Department, Albany, N.Y.*].

A married woman, even if she is under the compulsory school age of 16 years, who is living with her husband and maintaining the household, is not subject to the compulsory education laws and she need not attend school [*In re Rogers, 36 Misc. 2d 680 (Fam. Ct. Schuyler Co., 1962)*].

Remedy

If your school discriminates on the basis of sex, you should first speak to the principal about the discrimination. If you are not satisfied with the results, complain first to the local school superintendent, and then to the local Board of Education. You may seek review of an unfavorable decision either before the State Commissioner of Education [*Regulations of the Commis-*

sioner of Education §275] or before a court. In either case you will need a lawyer.

Federal law—Title IX

Federal legislation prohibits, with some exceptions, sex discrimination in the programs and activities of educational institutions receiving federal financial assistance, including any public or private preschool, elementary, or secondary school or institution of vocational, professional, or higher education [*Title IX of the Education Amendments of 1972, 20 U.S.C. §1681-1686 (1974), as amended 20 U.S.C. §1681 (1976 Supp.)*] Title IX does not apply to military schools or merchant marine academies [*20 U.S.C. §1681 (a) (4) (1974)*] or to educational institutions run by religious organizations if application of this title would be contrary to their religious beliefs [*20 U.S.C. §1681 (a) (3) (1974)*].

The following is a brief summary of the law's provisions:

Admissions: Title IX prohibits discrimination in admissions policies of vocational, professional and graduate schools, and in institutions of public undergraduate education [*20 U.S.C. §1681(a) (1) (1974)*], except for the few public undergraduate schools that have been traditionally and continually single sex [*20 U.S.C. §1681(a) (5) (1974)*]. The admissions provisions of Title IX do not apply to preschool, elementary, and secondary schools.

Curriculum: Once a school has admitted both sexes—whether its admissions policies are covered under Title IX or not—it must offer educational programs and activities on a non-discriminatory basis [*20 U.S.C. §1681(a) (1974)*]. Sex education classes and physical education class sessions which involve contact sports may be sex segregated [*45 CFR §86.34 (1975)*].

Pregnancy: Discrimination against female students because of pregnancy is prohibited. Full health services must include pregnancy and prenatal care, and a woman disabled by pregnancy must be treated like any other temporarily disabled person [*45 CFR §86.21(c), 86.39, 86.40 (1975)*].

Athletics: Title IX does not offer much protection against sex discrimination in athletics. Where selection is based on competitive skill or the activity involved is a contact sport, athletics may be provided either through separate teams for males and females or through a single team open to both sexes. Schools may prohibit women from participating on a male team in a contact sport. In non-contact sports, schools are permitted to maintain a single-sex team, provided members of the excluded sex are able to try out for membership; a separate team for women not able to make the male team need not be maintained. If athletic opportunities have not been limited in the past for women, a school may keep women from participating on men's teams regardless of whether the sport is contact or non-contact [45 CFR §86.41(b) (1975)]. The regulations require "equal athletic opportunity" for members of both sexes, but do not require equal expenditure of funds for male and female athletics programs [45 CFR §86.41(c) (1975)].

Scholarships: Discriminatory scholarship policies are outlawed by Title IX. Educational institutions, however, can maintain single-sex scholarships which are designated exclusively for one sex by will or trust as long as the total available scholarship money is granted equally to members of both sexes [45 CFR §86.37 (1975)].

Organizations: Schools receiving federal funds cannot sponsor or support organizations that discriminate by sex. The membership practices of certain voluntary youth service organizations and groups such as the Boy Scouts, Girl Scouts, Y.W.C.A., and Y.M.C.A. are not covered by Title IX [20 USC §1681(a) (6) (A) (1976 Supp.)].

Employment: The educational institutions covered by Title IX are prohibited from discriminating on the basis of sex in employment, including recruitment, advertising, hiring, promotion, and compensation [45 CFR §86.51 et seq. (1975)].* Educational institutions must provide equal pay for the same work to their male and female employees [45 CFR §86.54 (1975)]. An employer may not discriminate against or exclude from employment any employee or applicant on the basis of pregnancy, marital or parental status [45 CFR §86.57 (1975)].

Housing: Title IX does not prohibit educational institutions from maintaining separate living facilities for male and female students [20 U.S.C. §1686 (1974)]. However, such institutions

---

*One federal court has held that Title IX may not regulate employment at educational institutions. This case is now on appeal.

must provide housing of comparable cost and quality to members of both sexes [*45 CFR §86.32 (1975)*].

Remedy: Title IX violations

Complaints of Title IX violations should be made to:

Director, Office of Civil Rights
Department of Health, Education, and Welfare
330 Independence Avenue, S.W.
Washington, D.C. 20201

Civil Rights Act of 1964

Another federal statute which you might rely upon is the Civil Rights Act of 1964 [*Title IV of the 1964 Civil Rights Act, 42 U.S.C. §2000c et seq. (1974)*]. This Act was amended in 1972 to prohibit sex discrimination in public elementary and secondary schools and in public colleges, including technical or vocational schools above the secondary school level.

Remedy: Civil Rights Act violations

The Attorney General is authorized [*under 42 U.S.C. §2000c-6*] to initiate a lawsuit to remedy sex discrimination upon receipt of a written complaint:

1. signed by a parent or group of parents to the effect that their minor children are being deprived by a school board of the equal protection of the laws; or
2. signed by an individual, or her parent, to the effect that she has been denied admission to or not permitted to continue in attendance at a public college because of her sex.

The Attorney General must certify that the signer or signers of the complaint are unable to initiate and maintain appropriate legal proceedings (either because of the expense of the litigation or because the litigation would jeopardize their personal safety, employment, or economic standing) and that the lawsuit would further the orderly achievement of desegregation in public education [*42 U.S.C. §2000c-6 (1974)*].

Requests for lawsuits under this section should be addressed to:

Attorney General
Attention: Education Section
U.S. Department of Justice
10th Street and Pennsylvania Avenue, N.W.
Washington, D.C. 20530

It is not clear whether an individual has the right to file an action with her own lawyer under Title IV. Different courts have decided this question differently and at some point the issue will no doubt come before the Supreme Court.

Remedy: Constitutional violations

Besides violating state and federal law, sex discrimination by public educational institutions is unconstitutional. Complaints of constitutional violations may be brought in both state and federal court. You will need a lawyer to help you.

5. WELFARE

Welfare law is extremely complicated and a full discussion of it is beyond the scope of this pamphlet. You should know, however, that the various laws governing welfare and the court cases interpreting these laws do grant welfare recipients a number of important rights, which are frequently denied in practice by the welfare department. Therefore, you should get in touch with a welfare rights organization or legal services office (listed at the end of this section) to make sure that you do not lose your rights through ignorance.

Following is a very brief summary of some of the welfare laws that have a particular impact on women.

Types of welfare

There are two types of public assistance which a woman in New York State may receive if she is under 65 and not disabled:

Home Relief: Home Relief is aid provided to people unable to maintain themselves. This covers a woman who is not living with children [*Social Services Law §§131,157 et seq. (McKinney, 1976)*].

Aid to Dependent Children: A second category of welfare is Aid to Dependent Children (ADC) which provides financial assistance to:

1. Families with children under 18 years of age (or under 21 if the child attends school) [*Social Services Law §349 (McKinney 1976) 18 N.Y.C.R.R. §369*]. Children qualify for this if they are deprived of parental support or care because of the death, continued absence from the home, physical or mental incapacity, or in some cases, the unemployment [*18 N.Y.C.R.R. §369.2(7)*] of one or both parents;

2. Pregnant women who have no means of support [*Social Services Law §350(1) (f) (McKinney 1976); 18 N.Y.C.R.R. §§369.1, 369.2(a) (1), (f) (4)*]. A woman is entitled to a two-person grant and to medical care when the pregnancy is confirmed by medical diagnosis.

A woman on ADC whose children are six years of age or

older and who is able to work is required to participate in the Work Incentive Program (WIN) as a condition for receiving aid [*Social Services Law §350-e (McKinney 1976*]. If she fails or refuses to participate in WIN or turns down an offer of employment, her share of the ADC grant may be terminated [*Social Services Law §350-g (McKinney 1976*].

Food stamps, Medicaid and Social Services

In addition to a cash grant, recipients of public assistance are also entitled to receive food stamps [*7 CFR §271.3(b)*], Medicaid [*45 CFR §248.10*], and social services. Food stamps permit purchase of extra amounts of food; a Medicaid card provides payment for most medical services and prescriptions; and social services include provision of child care, homemakers, and other special services that are needed. Also, persons may apply for and receive food stamps, Medicaid, or social services separately if desired.

Father's duty to support

Fathers are legally required to support their children until the age of 21 [*Family Court §413 (McKinney 1975*]. Stepfathers are responsible for the support of their stepchildren under the age of 21 if the stepchildren are receiving public assistance or are in danger of doing so [*Social Services Law §101 (McKinney 1976); Family Court Act §415 (McKinney 1975)*]; or if they are patients in institutions run by the Department of Mental Hygiene [*Family Court Act §415 (McKinney 1975)*].

New York law authorizes the Department of Social Services to take steps to determine the paternity of children born out of wedlock, to locate absent fathers, and to determine the fathers' ability to contribute to the support of their children [*Social Services Law §352-a (McKinney 1976)*].

If you are on welfare, a welfare official may begin paternity proceedings in Family Court to determine who is the father of your child [*Family Court Act §522 (McKinney 1975)*] but only if the child is ten years or younger [*Family Court Act §517(b) (McKinney 1975)*]. If the court finds that a particular man is the father of your child, it may order him to make support payments for the child directly to the Department of Social Services or to the court [*Family Court Act §571(3) (McKinney 1975)*].

A woman who applies for welfare benefits for herself and her children must cooperate with the Department in identifying the father, establishing paternity and collecting support from the father. If she refuses to cooperate she can be refused welfare benefits for herself but not for her children [*18 N.Y.C.R.R. §351.2(2)(iv)*]. The Department may require a woman to give it the name of her child's father [*Social Services Law §349-b (McKinney Supp. 1976)*] and may refer ADC applicants to Family Court for paternity proceedings [*18 N.Y.C.R.R. f 369.2(3) (4)*].

Man in the house

Only the husband of a woman and the parents of a child are responsible for those persons' support. If a woman is living with a man who is not the father of any of her children and to whom she is not married, he is *not* responsible for her support or that of her children. A woman cannot be denied welfare because she is living with a man, and the man's income may not be taken into consideration in determining the amount of the woman's grant unless he is in fact paying rent or contributing to her support, in which case the amount he actually contributes can be deducted from the grant [*King v. Smith, 392 U.S. 309 (1968) affirming on other grounds 277 F. Supp. 31 (M.D. Ala. 1967)*].

How to apply

An applicant must go to her local welfare center to obtain an application form. The applications receptionist may not screen out persons who she thinks are ineligible. Everyone has the right to fill out a form and should insist on seeing the supervisor if refused a form. When you apply for assistance, you *must* be given a pamphlet which explains your rights to assistance, category of assistance and right to appeal any unjust decision or lack of decision in your case.

An application interview should normally be scheduled within five working days and in an emergency within an hour. Take the following documents with you: a) rent receipts; b) employment records, if any; c) marriage certificate; d) birth certificates or proof of age for everyone applying; e) social security cards [*18 N.Y.C.R.R. §351.5(a)*].

Refusal of application, reduction or discontinuance of grant

The welfare department must tell you if you are eligible for welfare within 30 days from the day you first asked for help. If they turn you down, they must give you a written statement of the reasons why they rejected you and you are entitled to a fair hearing, which you must request within sixty days [*Social Services Law §353 (McKinney 1976); 18 N.Y.C.R.R. §358.5(a)*].

If you are already on welfare, you must be given 15 days advance notice of any proposed action to terminate, suspend, or reduce your grant [*45 CFR §205.10; 18 N.Y.C.R.R. §358.8*]. If you request a fair hearing within the advance notice period, your assistance must be continued unchanged until a fair hearing decision is made by the Department of Social Services [*18 N.Y.C.R.R. §358.8(c)*].

You may request a fair hearing by writing to the New York State Department of Social Services, 1450 Western Avenue, Albany, N.Y. 12203; or by writing or going in person to the New York State Department of Social Services, Fair Housing Section, 80 Centre St. (First Floor), New York, N.Y. 10013; or by calling (212) 488-6550.

Supplemental Security Income

Supplementary Security Income (SSI) is a new federal program which is administered separately from the welfare programs described above by the Social Security Administration. It provides an income to all persons 65 years of age and over, and to the blind and disabled of any age who have limited income and resources [*Social Services Law §250 et seq. (McKinney 1976)*].

Resources

For information and help with welfare problems, get in touch with:

Community Action for Legal Services (CALS)
335 Broadway
New York, New York 10013
(212) 966-6600

(This is the central office which will refer you to a branch office in New York City or elsewhere in New York.) CALS also publishes a handbook on welfare titled "Manual for Welfare Advocates" available from the same office for $2.50 a copy.

In order to find out if you qualify for free assistance with welfare, Family Court or landlord tenant problems in New York City, contact one of the following offices:

MFY Legal Services
214 East 2nd Street
New York, N.Y.
(212) 777-5250
(MWF, 10 A.M.- 4 P.M.)
(handles cases from the East Side above Houston St.)

MFY Legal Services
759 10th Avenue
New York, N.Y.
(212) 581-2810
(handles cases from the West Side)

MFY Legal Services
95 Delancey Street
New York, N.Y.
(212) 533-8310
(handles cases from the area between Houston and Canal Streets)

MFY Legal Services
45 Canal Street
New York, N.Y.
(212) 966-7410
(handles cases from Chinatown)

6. DAYCARE

Families in New York who meet certain standards of financial and social need are entitled to receive free or low-cost daycare services for their children [*Title XX Social Security Act, 42 U.S.C. §1397 et seq. (1975 supp.), 18 NYCRR §394*].

Eligibility standards

Financial: Financial eligibility depends on the size of your income and the size of your family. The eligibility standards for residents of New York City differ from those applicable to residents of the rest of the state. Because both sets of standards change frequently they are not set forth here. To find out whether you are eligible for subsidized daycare you should consult your neighborhood Legal Services Office (see the end of this chapter for how to find the office).

Social need: If you are financially eligible for daycare, you must also have a "social need." You are considered to have a "social need" for daycare for your children if:

1. You are employed;
2. You are seeking employment, in which case you can put your child in a daycare center for 60 days while you look for a job. (One 50-day extension may be granted after which, if you are unsuccessful finding work, you are no longer eligible);
3. You are in a vocational training program for two years or less. (A lawsuit is now pending in federal court challenging the exclusion from daycare of children whose mothers are in four-year college programs. For information, call the Brooklyn Legal Services Office listed at the end of this section.)
4. You are sick or physically or emotionally incapacitated. This must be verified by your doctor or a social worker.

Hearings

You are entitled to a hearing if you are refused daycare. If your child is already in a daycare center, this hearing must take place before your child may be forced to leave [*45 CFR §228.14 (1974)*].

Resources

A full discussion of the law concerning daycare is beyond the scope of this pamphlet. In New York City, for further information and help with problems involving daycare, contact:

Brooklyn Legal Services Corp.
152 Court Street
Brooklyn, N.Y. 11201
(212) UL 5-8003

Bank Street Daycare Consultation Service
610 West 112th Street
New York, N.Y. 10025
(212) 663-7200

In upstate New York, call your local legal services office for information.

7. CREDIT

Credit is defined as the right conferred upon a person by any lender to incur a debt and postpone its payment, whether or not any interest or finance charge is imposed.

Federal, state, and New York City laws prohibit discrimination based on sex or marital status in credit lending [*Equal Credit Opportunity Act, Title VII, 15 U.S.C. §1691-1691(e) (1975 Supp.); N.Y. Executive Law §296-a (McKinney Supp. 1976); N.Y.C. Admin. Code, §B1-7.0 (5) (d) (1975 Suppl.)*]. They assure legal access to credit for women who would qualify but for their sex or marital status.

Who is entitled to credit

The protection of the credit laws only applies to people who have income or assets of their own sufficient to establish credit. A married woman with her own income or assets is entitled to her own credit account or she may prefer a joint account with her husband. A wife with no income or assets of her own is not entitled to her own account, but may use her husband's account if the creditor offers such "courtesy" privileges. For example, many women with no income or assets of their own who would not qualify for a credit card, may use their husband's card as a "courtesy." In either case, if a woman has a joint account or uses her husband's account she has the right to create her own credit history. Under the provisions of the Federal Equal Credit Opportunity Act [*12 CFR Sections 202.10(a) (b) (1977)*] a woman can require a creditor who reports information on such accounts to credit bureaus to report it in both names. This will cause the credit bureau to establish a separate file for each spouse and thereby create a credit history for both. Married, divorced, separated or widowed women should check all their family credit accounts to be sure that information is being reported in their individual names and should contact their local credit bureaus to be sure that a file is maintained in their own names. Thus established, an individual credit history of a woman who uses her husband's accounts but has no income or assets of her own, may not be sufficient by itself to satisfy requirements for an independent credit account, but it certainly will help.

New York State law

The State Human Rights Law *(Executive Law §296-a (McKinney Supp. 1976)]* makes the following practices by a creditor unlawful.

A creditor may not:

1. Grant, withold, renew or fix rates and conditions on the basis of an applicant's sex or marital status in applications for credit for acquisitions, construction, rehabilitation, repair, and maintenance of housing accommodations. [*The new Federal Housing Act (See section on housing) specifically prohibits discrimination in granting federally-related home mortgage loans.*]
2. Grant, withold, extend, renew, or fix rates, terms or conditions of, any form of credit on the basis of sex or marital status.
3. Use a credit application or make any inquiry which indicates any limitation, specification or discrimination on the basis of sex or marital status.
4. Ask questions concerning a woman's birth control method, family planning, and capacity to bear children.
5. Refuse to consider sources of income (e.g. alimony) or to discount all or part of a woman's income on the basis of sex or marital status.
6. Require that a newly married woman with a credit history reapply for credit as a new applicant.
7. Refuse to extend credit to a credit-worthy woman in her own legal (maiden) name.
8. Adjust a credit rating on the basis of a husband's individual credit rating.
9. Refuse to maintain a separate credit history for a married or divorced woman who requests in writing that this be done.

Credit decisions are not considered discriminatory if they are based on a woman's current income, assets, prior credit history and other data, as long as these criteria apply equally to male applicants. A woman who is denied credit should request a statement from the creditor of the specific reasons for the denial. The law requires that reasons be provided [*Executive Law §296(a) 4(b) (McKinney Supp. 1975)*]. If the information on which the denial of credit is based is incorrect or out-of-date, you may ask that it be reinvestigated and add your own statement to the file.

New York City law

While New York City has no law specifically prohibiting credit discrimination except in the purchase, repair, or maintenance of housing, land, or commercial space [*N.Y.C. Admin. Code, Chap. 1, Title B, §B1-7.0 (5)(d)*], the City Commission on Human Rights has determined that the prohibition against discrimination in public accommodations [*Administrative Code Section B1-7.0.(2) (1972)*] covers creditors and the Commission will accept some complaints of credit discrimination. Most credit complaints, however, are referred to the State Division of Human Rights.

Remedies

Under State law, a woman who has been denied credit because of her sex or marital status can file a complaint within one year in one of three places.

(1) The most effective place to file is the *State Division of Human Rights* (although if the discrimination took place in New York City, you may also file at the City Human Rights Commission). [*see section on Procedures*]. If either agency finds discrimination, it may order that credit be granted and money damages paid to the aggrieved woman [*Executive Law §297 (McKinney Supp. 1976)*].

(2) Complaints may also be filed with the *Superintendent of Banking* within a year after the discriminatory act has taken place. If the Superintendent finds probable cause to believe that discrimination has occurred, he will attempt to aid the creditor and the woman to reach an agreement; if this fails a hearing will be held at which the woman has a right to be represented by a lawyer. If the Superintendent finds proof of discrimination at the hearing he has the power to order that credit be granted and money damages paid [*Executive Law Section 296-a (7) (McKinney Supp. 1976)*].

(3) Finally, a creditor who discriminates may be sued in court for damages and other relief [*Executive Law §297(9) (McKinney Supp. 1976)*]. This method is slow and can be expensive.

Remember, you can pursue *only one* of these remedies. Once you have filed your complaint in one place you cannot then file it in another [*Executive Law §§296-a(6), 297(9) (McKinney Supp. 1976)*].

Federal law

The Equal Credit Opportunity Act [*15 U.S.C. Section 1691-1691e (1975 Supp.)*] prohibits discrimination on the basis of sex or marital status in any aspect of a credit transaction. The act and its implementing regulations [*12 CFR Section 202 (1977)*] provide:

(1) A creditor may inquire about an applicant's marital status *only* for the purpose of ascertaining the creditor's rights and responsibilities in regard to that particular extension of credit [*15 U.S.C. Section 1691*].

(2) A creditor may request the signatures of both parties of a marriage if required by state law to create a valid lien, to pass clear title, to waive inchoate rights to property, or to assign earnings [*15 U.S.C. Section 1691d(a)*].

(3) A creditor shall not refuse on the basis of sex or marital status to grant a separate account to a creditworthy applicant [*12 CFR Section 202.7(a)*].

(4) A creditor shall not prohibit an applicant from opening or maintaining an account in a birth-given first name and surname or a birth-given first name and a combined surname [*12 CFR §202.7(b)*].

(5) Where an applicant chooses to disclose alimony, child support, or maintenance payments, a creditor shall consider such payments as income to the extent that such payments are likely to be consistently made [*12 CFR Section 202.6(b) (5)*].

(6) A creditor shall not discount the income of an applicant or applicant's spouse on the basis of sex or marital status. A creditor shall not discount income solely because it is derived from part-time employment, but may consider the probable continuity of such income in evaluating the creditworthiness of an applicant [*12 CFR §202.6(b) (5)*].

(7) A creditor shall not request information about birth control practices or childbearing intentions or capabilities [*12 CFR §202.5(d) (4)*].

(8) Except where credit is based solely upon income earned by an applicant's spouse, a creditor shall not on the basis of a change in name or marital status [*12 CFR §202.7(e)*]:
(a) require a reapplication
(b) require a change in the terms of the account
(c) terminate the account.

(9) Married persons have the right to have credit information concerning joint accounts reported to consumer reporting agencies and creditors in the names of both husband and wife [*12 CFR §202.10(a) (b)*].

Remedies

If a creditor discriminates against you, under federal law you can complain or sue in one of two places.

Administrative agencies: The Equal Credit Opportunity Act is enforced by different federal agencies, depending upon the type of creditor who engaged in the discriminatory practice. When credit is denied, the creditor must furnish the name and address of the correct enforcing agency. You can also call or write the Federal Trade Commission, 26 Federal Plaza, New York, N.Y., (212) 264-1207, which has overall authority to enforce compliance with the Act [*15 U.S.C. §1691c(c)*] and they will tell you the correct agency to contact. The FTC does not represent individuals.

Federal Court: If a creditor discriminates against you, you may sue in a federal district court within one year of the discrimination. If you are successful, the court will order the creditor to pay court costs and your attorney's fees in addition to money for any actual damage you have suffered. The court may also award punitive damages or issue an injunction [*15 U.S.C. §1691e (a) (b) (c)*]. You may not sue under the federal law in addition to seeking remedies under New York State or local laws [*15 U.S.C. §1691d(e)*].

References

Pamphlet: Equal Credit Opportunity Act (free). Write to:

Federal Trade Commission
Legal & Public Records, Room 130
Washington, D.C. 20580

8. TAXES

Although the Federal tax law does not discriminate in express terms against women, there are many ways in which it may place a married woman at a serious disadvantage.

Single or joint returns

A marriage in which a husband and wife earn approximately equal wages is heavily taxed. When a married woman is earning much less than her husband, the couple benefits from filing a joint income tax return. If their earnings are equivalent, or nearly so, their tax burden is disproportionate to that of single wage earners regardless of what method of filing they choose. [*Int. Rev. Code, §1(a)-(d)*].

Standard deduction

At present two single persons pay less tax than many two-earner couples with the same total income. One cause of the differential is the standard deduction. Each single taxpayer is entitled to take a standard deduction, but when two taxpayers join in marriage, one standard deduction is lost. [*Int. Rev. Code, §141(b)*].

Divorce costs

Legal or accountant's fees for tax planning in divorce actions are deductible, although legal fees for representation in the divorce are not deductible. Also, if you get a divorce on or before the last day of the tax year, you are considered single for that entire tax year. [*Int. Rev. Code, §143*].

Alimony

Periodic alimony payments (of a fixed sum paid over an indefinite period) are deductible by the husband paying the alimony and includable as taxable income by the wife receiving them [*Int. Rev. Code, §§71(a), (d), 215 (a)*]. Lump-sum alimony is generally neither deductible by the person paying nor taxable to the person receiving it if the lump-sum installments occur over 10 years or less [*Int. Rev. Code, §71 (c)*]. When installments cover 10 years or more, they are considered periodic payments (like alimony) and are therefore deductible by the husband paying and taxable to the wife receiving payment [*Int. Rev. Code, §71 (c) (2)*].

Child support

Child support payments are not deductible by the parent paying support or includable as income for the parent who has custody [*Int. Rev. Code, §71 (b)*]. There is a presumption in favor of the custodial parent that the child is that parent's dependent, if the child resides with that parent for most of the year [*Int. Rev. Code §152 (e) (1)*]. (The IRS then considers that the custodial parent, normally the mother, has contributed more than half the "support" for the child, and thus is entitled to a dependent exemption.) However, the parent who does not have physical custody of the child may be specifically entitled to the exemption, if:

1. s/he contributed more than $600 toward the child's support during the calendar year; and
2. under the decree of dissolution, or written agreement between the parties, that parent is given the right to take the exemption [*Int. Rev. Code, §152 (e) (2) (A)*].

If the noncustodial parent provided $1,200 or more in support for the child/ren for the calendar year, the custodial parent must "clearly establish" that s/he provided more for the support of the child/ren [*Int. Rev. Code, §152 (e) (2) (B)*]. Each parent, if the question of support is contested, must submit itemized statements of what was actually spent on the child/ren. Thus, a woman who has custody must keep precise and accurate records of money spent on the child/ren. Because the $1,200 figure is constant, regardless of the number of children, the noncustodial parent, normally the father, could spend $300 per year for each of four children and still get an exemption of $750 per child, or $3,000.

Problems can often be avoided by splitting the exemptions; that is, the father and mother in a family of four children may agree that each will claim exemptions for two of the children. The mother would probably find it profitable to take an exemption for the youngest child becaue it will apply for the longest time and the mother will be eligible for the child care tax credit.

Child care tax credit

A taxpayer who supports a child under 15 years of age or a physically or mentally handicapped spouse or other relative, is eligible for a tax credit equal to 20 percent of her employment related expenses (i.e. expenses for household services and for care of the child or other dependent) if these expenses are incurred to enable her to be gainfully employed [*Int. Rev. Code §44A (a)*]. * After the tax liability has been calculated, the amount of tax owed is reduced by the amount of the credit. The tax credit may be taken whether you itemize deductions or use the standard deduction.

The statute limits the amount of the tax credit by providing that the amount of employment-related expenses on which the credit is based may not exceed $2,000 for one dependent or $4,000 for two or more dependents [*Int. Rev. Code, §44A (d)*]. Furthermore, for purposes of calculating the tax credit, the employment-related expenses of an unmarried taxpayer may not exceed her earned income for the year; for a married taxpayer the employment-related expenses may not exceed her earned income or that of her spouse, whichever is less [*Int. Rev. Code, §44A (c)*].

Married couples *must* file a joint return to qualify for the tax credit. A taxpayer who is divorced or legally separated from her spouse or who has lived apart from her spouse for the last 6 months of the year and has maintained a household where her child lives is not considered married for purposes of the tax credit provision. If the parents of a child are divorced and one parent has custody of the child for over one-half of the year, only that parent can claim the child care tax credit [*Int. Rev. Code, §44A (f)*].

Medical deductions

Expenses for contraceptives, abortions and sterilizations are now deductible as ordinary medical expenses [*Int. Rev. Code §213*]. Also, transportation to the hospital to visit a sick child or spouse is deductible at 6¢ per mile, with the proper supporting records.

---

*See appendix to Chapter 8.

Remedy

If you have questions, or need help filling out tax forms, you can contact any IRS office. A public-interest law reform organization in this field is Tax Analysts and Advocates, 732 17th St., N.W., Washington, D.C. 20006.

References

An article describing tax advantages as well as disadvantages for the married gainfully-employed woman, written by Tax Court Judge Cynthia Holcomb Hall, "The Working Woman and the Federal Income Tax," appears in Volume 61 of the American Bar Association Journal at page 716 (June 1975).

Tax assistance

To obtain tax forms or free assistance in preparing your state tax returns, call or write:

New York State Income Tax Section
2 World Trade Center
New York, N.Y. 10047
(212) 488-3400

To obtain assistance in preparing New York City tax returns, call or write

New York City Income Tax Section
2 World Trade Center, Room 6379
New York, N.Y. 10047
(212) 964-5900

To obtain New York City tax forms, call (212) 966-3025.

9. SOCIAL SECURITY

Who is eligible for benefits

All gainfully employed women are entitled to Social Security benefits in their own right [*42 U.S.C. §402*]. The Social Security tax on your wages is payable half by you, half by your employer. You should make sure your employer has your correct Social Security number and is reporting your wages to the Internal Revenue Service. Household workers should insist that their employers report their income so that they can receive Social Security benefits.

Women wage earners: As a worker, you are entitled to benefits:

1. if you become disabled and are unable to be gainfully employed after the age of 31 and if you worked 5 out of the 10 years preceding the disability;

2. when you reach 65 years or 62 on the early retirement option, on the basis of your earnings. Since these benefits are often larger than disability benefits, it may be better to retire at 62 if you are receiving disability benefits.

Wives: As the wife of a worker, you are entitled to:

1. retirement benefits on his account equal to ½ of his monthly benefits when he retires and you reach the age of 62. Monthly sums will be larger if you wait until you are 65;

2. benefits for yourself and your children until the youngest is 18 or is over 18 and disabled if you are caring for the children at the time of his death, retirement or disability.

3. A widow's pension at the age of 60, or age 50 if you are disabled, even if you have no children.

4. a lump sum death benefit if you were living with your husband at the time of his death (in addition to the above).

Divorced women

A divorced woman is also entitled to draw benefits on her former husband's account if she was married to him for at least 20 years and has not remarried. You may want to get a separation order rather than a divorce if you have been married less than 20 years, so that you can receive the benefits. (See section on marriage and divorce.)

Election of benefits

Married women wage earners are not entitled to receive both their own benefits and their husbands'. Rather they must claim either one benefit or the other. Since the computation of a worker's benefits is based on the average salary earned during the working years it may be advantageous for women, who have historically been underpaid, to elect to receive benefits as dependents of their husbands rather than in their own right as wage earners.

Housewives

Women who work at home doing domestic chores and raising children are not entitled to receive their own Social Security benefits. Rather they are entitled to collect benefits only through their husbands.

References

There are many sexual inequities in the Social Security law. Sex-based differentials in Social Security are discussed in detail in "Report of the 1974 Advisory Council on Social Security" [*Appendix B: Report of the Subcommittee on Treatment of Men and Women (with respect to sex and marital status), pp. 171-202*]. For copies write to Department of Health, Education and Welfare, 330 Independence Avenue, S.W., Washington, D.C. 20201.

10. INSURANCE

New York State law prohibits discrimination on the basis of sex and marital status in the sale of any type of insurance [*Insurance Law, Section 40-e (McKinney Supp. 1976)*].* This means that any insurance policy offered for sale in New York to males must also be made available to similarly situated females. An insurance company may not provide one set of terms for women and another for men. The law also prohibits insurance companies from cancelling or refusing to renew policies because of the sex or marital status of a policyholder [*Insurance Law, §40-e (McKinney Supp. 1976)*]. An insurance company may, however, charge different rates for women and men if they are based on valid actuarial statistics reflecting the differing risk of insuring women and men.

New York City has no specific law prohibiting discrimination in insurance, but the City Commission on Human Rights has determined that the law prohibiting sex discrimination in public accommodations applies to insurers and the Commission will hear complaints of sex discrimination in insurance.

Individual insurance

It is important to note that any women who are "similarly situated" to men are entitled to identical insurance. Thus, while it is unlawful for an insurance company to refuse to sell a special "gold star" disability insurance policy to a woman lawyer that it offers to a male lawyer, it is not unlawful to refuse to sell disability insurance to a housewife who earns no money since a househusband would also be denied such insurance.

Group insurance plans

Group insurance plans are also prohibited from discriminating on the basis of sex and marital status [*Insurance Law, §40-e (McKinney Supp. 1976)*]. If an employer provides unequal insurance coverage to his male and female employees he can be charged with sex discrimination in employment at the

---

*See appendix to Chapter 10.

Human Rights Commission and the Equal Employment Opportunity Commission (see chapters on Employment and Procedures). New York law also requires that a woman disabled by pregnancy is entitled to receive disability benefits (see Chapter on Employment).

Maternity care coverage

A recent New York State law requires that individual and group insurance policies which provide hospital, surgical or medical care must provide coverage for maternity care [*Insurance Law, §§162-a, 164-a (McKinney Supp. 1976)*].* However, maternity care coverage, except for coverage for complications of pregnancy, may be limited to four days of hospital confinement and only covers women who have been insured for ten months. This law does not cover government employees. It is unclear whether the law covers abortion expenses. The law went into effect on January 1, 1977, and as written, applies to insurance policies written, amended, or renewed on or after that date. As of this writing, a lawsuit is pending challenging this law. It is also unclear whether insurance companies may refuse to cover a single woman who purchases individual (rather than family) coverage for abortion and maternity expenses. If you are denied such coverage, call the Civil Liberties Union.

Remedy

Complaints concerning discrimination in insurance should be made to the State Division of Human Rights or the New York City Commission on Human Rights (if the discrimination took place in New York City), and the Department of Insurance at:

State Division of Human Rights
2 World Trade Center
New York, New York 10047; or

New York City Commission on Human Rights
52 Duane Street
New York, New York 10007

Department of Insurance
Agency Building #1
Empire State Plaza
Albany, New York 11223.

---

*See appendix to Chapter 10.

Before filing a complaint, it may be worthwhile to call these new laws to the attention of the offending insurance companies or agents, many of whom simply have never heard of them.

11. HOUSING

Federal, State and New York City laws prohibit discrimination against women in housing on the basis of sex or marital status.

Federal law

Title VIII of the Civil Rights Act of 1968 prohibits discrimination on the basis of sex in the sale, rental, or finance of housing or land [*42 U.S.C. §§3601-3619, 3631 (1973), as amended 42 U.S.C. §3604-3606 (Supp. 1976)*]. No owner or agent may refuse to sell, rent or sublet any dwelling or land or claim that any dwelling is not available for inspection, sale, or rental when it is in fact available. It is also illegal to publish a notice, statement, or advertisement which indicates any preference or discrimination on the basis of sex or to discriminate in the provision of services or facilities in connection with the sale or rental of dwellings or land [*42 U.S.C. §3604 (Supp. 1976), amending 42 U.S.C. §3604 (1973)*]. The following types of housing are exempted from this law:

1. any single-family house sold or rented by an owner, provided the house is sold or rented without the services of a real estate broker, agent or salesman [*42 U.S.C. §3603(b) (1973)*].
2. rooms or units in a dwelling containing living quarters for not more than four families if the owner actually lives there [*42 U.S.C. §3603(b) (1973)*].

The law also permits a religious organization to limit the sale, rental, or occupancy of dwellings which it owns to persons of the same religion and allows a private club which provides lodgings to limit or to give preference to its own members in the rental or occupancy of such lodgings [*42 U.S.C. §3607 (1973)*].

No bank, building and loan association, insurance company or other corporation which makes commercial real estate loans may deny a loan for purchasing, constructing, or repairing a dwelling or discriminate in the amount, interest rate, or other terms and conditions of a loan on the basis of sex [*42 U.S.C. §3605 (Supp. 1976), amending 42 U.S.C. §3606 (1973)*]. It is also illegal for a real estate broker to discriminate in providing services [*42 U.S.C. §3606 (Supp. 1976), amending 42 U.S.C. §3606 (1973)*].

The Housing and Community Development Act of 1974 provides federal funds for community development programs designed to eliminate or prevent slums and to improve community facilities, including the provision of supporting health, social and other services [*42 U.S.C. §§5301-5317 (Suppl. 1976)*]. Section 109 prohibits discrimination on the basis of sex in any program funded under this Act [*42 U.S.C §5309 (Supp. 1976)*].

New York State and City law

It is unlawful for an owner or other person (e.g. rental agent, real estate broker) authorized to sell, rent or lease housing accommodations, land or commercial space, to discriminate on the basis of sex or marital status [*Exec. Law §296(5) (McKinney 1972), as amended Exec. Law §296 (McKinney Supp. 1976) N.Y.C. Admin. Code Chap. 1, Title B §B1-7.0(3) (Supp. 1976)*]. No advertisement, statement or application form for purchase or rental may limit availability of housing or land on the basis of sex or discourage women from seeking to purchase or rent such property. Exceptions to both State and City laws are:

1. Housing in a two-family building in which the owner and his or her family is one of those families, or
2. If the rental of a room is by the occupant of the house or apartment, or
3. If the building is entirely restricted to one sex (boarding house).

Discrimination against families with children

It is unlawful under State law for a landlord to refuse rental of an apartment or other dwelling (in a city) because he or she does not want children on the premises [*Landlord-Tenant Act, Real Property Law §236 (McKinney 1968)*].

Remedies

Title VIII: Complaints of sex discrimination under Title VIII should be filed with the Secretary of the Housing and Urban Development Agency within 180 days after the discriminatory housing practice occurred [*42 U.S.C. §3610 (1973)*]. You may either go to one of the following offices or call and ask to have a complaint form sent to you:

Regional office:

HUD, Equal Opportunity Office
26 Federal Plaza, 35th Floor, Rm. 3502
New York, N.Y. 10007
(212) 264-1759

Area offices:

HUD
665 Fifth Avenue
New York, N.Y. 10019

HUD
Leo W. O'Brien Federal Building
North Pearl and Clinton Avenue
Albany, New York 12207

HUD
Grant Building
560 Main Street
Buffalo, New York 14202

The Act provides that complaints be turned over to the State or City Human Rights Agency for initial action [*42 U.S.C. §3610 (c) (1973)*]. However, the New York Regional office is currently handling all complaints itself because of administrative backlogs in the state and local agencies. The HUD Secretary will investigate the complaint within 30 days. If he decides to resolve it, he will try to correct or eliminate the discriminatory practice by the informal methods of conference, conciliation, and persuasion [*42 U.S.C. §3610(a) (1973)*].

If the Secretary is unable to resolve the complaint, you may bring suit in federal or state court within 180 days after the discriminatory practice occurred, but you will need a lawyer [*42*

U.S.C. §§3610(d), 3612 (1973)]. If you win the suit, the court may require the defendant to pay your attorney's fees if you are unable to do so [42 U.S.C. §3612(c) (1973)]. The court may also grant an injunction against the discriminatory practice and award you money for any actual damages you have suffered and up to $1,000 in punitive damages [42 U.S.C. §3612 (c) (1973)].

Housing and Community Development Act: Complaints of violations of the Housing and Community Development Act should also be made to a HUD office.

State law: Complaints of violations of state law should be brought directly to the State Division of Human Rights. (See Section on Procedure).

Discrimination against families with children: Complaints of discrimination against families with children should be filed with the Clerk of the Criminal Court. Because a landlord's reason for refusal to rent may be difficult to prove, you may want to take a friend with you when looking for housing so that he or she may witness the conversation.

12. PUBLIC ACCOMMODATIONS

Under New York State law, no person may be refused access to any public accommodation, or prevented from taking advantage of any of the privileges of such facilities, on the basis of sex or marital status [*N.Y. Human Rights Law, Executive Law §296 (2) (McKinney Supp. 1976) (amending Executive Law §296 (2) 1972)*]. Any advertisement or notice which indicates that a woman's presence and patronage would be unwelcome and unacceptable is also an unlawful practice.

Public accommodations include such places as hotels, restaurants, stores, swimming pools, theaters, pool halls, all public conveyances, and such services as insurance and extension of credit. The term does not include public libraries, schools (which are covered by other State law—see Education section) or places obviously private in nature (private clubs). An illustration of unlawful discrimination is the refusal of a cocktail lounge to admit unescorted women into the establishment, while allowing unescorted males to enter.

The Human Rights Law does not prevent the exclusion of members of one sex from public accommodations when the failure to do so would result in invasions of physical privacy [*Executive Law §296 (2) (b)*]. For example, public restrooms and locker rooms may be sex-segregated.

The New York City Human Rights Law also protects women against discrimination in public accommodations on the basis of sex, but does not prohibit discrimination on the basis of marital status *(N.Y.C. Admin. Code Chap. 1, Title B §B1-7.0 (2) (Supp. 1976)]*.

A woman who is refused access to a public accommodation, resort or amusement, should file a complaint with the New York State Division of Human Rights as outlined in the section on Procedures. In New York City, she may also file with the City Commission on Human Rights.

13. JURY DUTY

State Court

Women have the same obligation to serve on juries in New York State courts as do men [*Judiciary Law §507 (McKinney 1975)*]. An exemption from jury duty is provided to any person of either sex who has the responsibility of caring for a child under 16 years old during the day, excluding the hours the child is in school [*Judiciary Law §512 (McKinney 1977)*].

Federal Court

Although the Federal Judiciary Law lists no jury duty exemptions, a woman caring for a young child is permitted to claim an exemption from jury duty [*Court Plans for the New York Federal Courts*]. The Northern and Western District Courts grant exemptions to women with legal custody of children under 10 years old. The Southern District exempts women with children under 12 years old and the Eastern District women with children under 16 years old.

14. MARRIAGE AND DIVORCE

Marriage requirements

Age: In New York State, a woman may marry at the age of 14 and a man at 16 [*Domestic Relations Law §15-a*] but persons under 18 must have written parental consent to the marriage [*Dom. Rel. Law §15(2)*] and a woman under 16 must also have the approval of a Family Court or Supreme Court judge [*Dom. Rel. Law §15(3)*].

Blood test: Both partners must have a blood test no later than 10 days and no more than 30 days before the marriage [*Dom. Rel. Law §13-a*].

License: A marriage license must be obtained no later than 24 hours before the ceremony. Once the license is obtained, the marriage must take place within 60 days or the license becomes void [*Dom. Rel. Law §13-b*].

Types of marriage

Ceremonial: This is the most common type of marriage. Both parties declare to a person authorized by law to perform marriages their intention to enter into the marriage relationship. At least one witness besides the person performing the ceremony is required [*Dom. Rel. Law §12*].

Contractual: It is possible in New York State to dispense with a wedding ceremony and simply to sign and acknowledge a "marriage contract" before a judge of a court of record in New York State and two witnesses (who must also sign and acknowledge it) and then file it with the County Clerk. The contract simply states the names and addresses of the parties and their intent to marry [*Dom. Rel. Law §11*].

No common law marriage: Common law marriage means that a couple is automatically considered legally married once they have lived together for a specified number of years. New York State does *not* recognize any common law marriage entered into after 1933 except in a very few situations, such as when a couple has moved to New York from a state that does recognize such marriages. Since a woman is not entitled to various benefits, such as her husband's Social Security benefits, if she is not legally married, it is important that she consult a lawyer if there is any doubt about her marital status.

Obligations of marriage

A husband has the legal duty to support his wife [*Dom. Rel. Law §32*]. If a husband refuses to support his wife, she can petition the Family Court for an order of support [*Dom. Rel. Law §37*].

If a husband is disabled, his wife is legally liable for his support. Both parties are liable for the support of their children under 21 (and over 21 if the child is unable to maintain him or herself) [*Dom. Rel. Law §32*].

Ante-nuptial agreements

Occasionally couples enter into legal agreements before they are married providing for such things as property settlements when one or the other spouse dies. These agreements are legally enforceable as long as they do not violate public policy. It is important to note, however, that the law does not consider marriage to be simply a private agreement between a man and a woman, and no provision in a marriage contract will be enforced if it is contrary to New York laws governing marriage. For example, a couple may agree that the wife will support the husband and he will do the housework, but no court will enforce the agreement should one of the parties have a change of heart, because New York law requires husbands to support their wives.

Divorce

"No fault" divorce: If a husband and wife simply don't love each other any more or aren't getting along, they can get divorced by signing and filing with the county clerk a separation agreement and living apart for one year abiding by its terms. At the end of a year, a divorce will be granted by a court almost automatically unless the couple reconciles or one party to the agreement claims the other didn't live up to its terms or tricked the spouse into signing it or forced him or her to sign it. Usually separation agreements divide property and provide for alimony and child custody. The terms of the separation agreement are generally incorporated into the divorce decree, so it is an important document and should be drawn up with the help of a lawyer [*Dom. Rel. Law §170*].

Decree of separation: Sometimes, for various reasons, people choose to enter into a legal separation instead of getting divorced. They do this by means of a decree or judgment of separation. Unlike a separation agreement, a decree of separation is granted by a court rather than simply being agreed on by the spouses. The grounds for getting a decree or judgment of separation are the same as those for a divorce, except that abandonment as a grounds for divorce must be for one year, while as a grounds for separation, simple abandonment for any length of time is sufficient. Further, a wife can get a judgment of separation on grounds of non-support by the husband. At the end of a year, either party can sue for divorce, no matter who was at fault, provided that there is proof of substantial compliance with the provisions of the separation judgment [*Dom. Rel. Law §170*].

Annulment

Annulment is different from divorce or legal separation in that a divorce or legal separation presumes that a valid marriage existed, whereas annulment assumes that the marriage was invalid in the first place. There are two types of marriages that can be annulled:

Void marriages: A marriage is void and by law *must* be annulled if it is:

1. *Incestuous:* parent/child; grandparent/grandchild; brother/sister [*Dom. Rel. Law §5*]. Aunt/nephew; uncle/niece marriages may not be performed in New York but will be considered valid if entered into in a state that permits them.
2. *Bigamous:* either party is legally married to someone else [*Dom. Rel. Law §6*].
3. The former husband or wife has been finally sentenced to *life imprisonment* [*Dom. Rel. Law §6*].

Voidable marriages: A voidable marriage is considered valid while it exists, but may be annulled at the request of one of the parties. A marriage *may* be annulled if:

1. it was entered to by means of *force, duress or fraud;*
2. one of the parties had at the time of the marriage an *in-*

curable physical incapacity that would prevent the couple from having sexual relations;

3. there was some sort of *mental incapacity* that at the time of the marriage prevented one party from understanding the nature of the marriage relationship; or

4. one party is incurably *insane for 5 years* after the marriage; or

5. one party was *under 18 years old* at the time of the marriage. (Annulment on this ground is at the discretion of the court which will take into consideration the facts and circumstances of the marriage.)

There are different time limitations for each of the different grounds after which an annulment may not be granted [*Dom. Rel. Law §7*].

Dissolution by presumption of death

A final way of dissolving a marriage under New York law is by showing that a spouse has been missing for five consecutive years; that diligent, unsuccessful search has been made; and that it is reasonable to believe he or she is dead (e.g., went down on the Titanic. It would not be sufficient to state simply that the last you heard from him he was in Las Vegas) [*Dom. Rel. Law §221*].

Property

Ownership: Usually the question of which spouse owns what property does not arise until a couple is divorced. At that stage too many women are horrified to discover for the first time that because their husbands paid for everything, they own everything except gifts, clothes and personal items which belong to the wife. Property law is very complicated, and which spouse owns what property depends on the type of property involved. If you are contemplating divorce, it is imperative to consult a lawyer about an equitable property division.

New York is a common law property state. This means that as a general rule, personal property acquired during marriage belongs to the person who bought it or to whom it was given as a gift, and real property belongs to the person who holds the title to it, no matter who paid for it. Joint bank accounts and jointly owned stocks probably belong to the spouse who deposited the money or bought the stocks, although when a joint bank account is opened payable to A or B or the survivor, the law presumes a gift of ½ of the sum by the person who opened the account to the other. This presumption may be rebutted by proof that it was not intended to be a gift but was put in that form for convenience only.

Possession: Even if a divorcing wife finds herself owning no property, a court may award her possession of property. For example, she may be permitted to live in the couple's former home, even though the husband is the legal owner. This is usually the case where the wife is awarded custody of the couple's minor children.

Alimony

In New York, alimony may be awarded only to needy wives, not needy husbands. [*Dom. Rel. Law §236*].

Temporary alimony may be awarded to a wife while any matrimonial action is pending. The amount is determined only on the basis of the wife's need and the husband's assets. Fault is almost always irrelevant.

Permanent alimony is awarded at the time a divorce or separation is granted. The amount of the award depends not only on the need of the wife and the finances of the husband, but also on such factors as the length of the marriage, the standard of living of the parties before they separated, who was at fault, and the ability of the wife to support herself.* If a wife is found guilty of such misconduct as would entitle her husband to a divorce or separation, she is barred from receiving any alimony. Alimony must cease when a wife remarries or a husband dies, unless the parties agreed otherwise in a separation agreement. If the circumstances of the parties change, the court can order a change in the amount of alimony, unless there is a separation agreement providing otherwise, incorporated in the divorce decree. In this case, if a wife is, or is likely to become, a public charge, additional alimony may be granted by the court.

Child custody

If a couple cannot decide who should have custody of their under-age (minor) children, a court will award custody on the basis of what it considers the best interests of the child.

---

*See appendix to Chapter 14.

Although in the past, child custody was almost invariably awarded to the mother unless she was proven to be unfit, today the presumption in favor of the mother is changing and a woman must be prepared to prove that it is in fact in the best interests of the child to live with her. Child custody is never permanent and can be changed by the court in accordance with the interests of the child. Under New York law, both parents have equal right to custody [*Dom. Rel. Law §70 and §240*]. The fact that a woman is a lesbian does not automatically make her legally unfit to have custody of the child/ren.

Child support

In New York, a father is primarily liable for the support of the couple's children; a mother is only secondarily liable.

15. NAME CHANGE

In New York State a woman's name does *not* change automatically to that of her husband when she marries. There is nothing in the marriage ceremony or marriage license which changes a wife's name. The practice is only a custom. If you wish to keep your own name when you marry, just keep using it; it is your "legal" name.

If you did change your name when you got married and want to change it back again, you should start using your own name consistently. Inform everyone, such as banks, stores in which you have charge accounts, the Motor Vehicles Bureau, Social Security, etc. that henceforth you will be known by your birth name for all purposes. It is perfectly lawful for anyone to change his or her name to anything at all as long as the change is not for a fraudulent purpose, such as avoiding creditors.

Women who retain or regain their own names often find that banks, landlords, employers, licensing agencies, and stores refuse to provide services unless they use their husband's names. Some women find that their names have been altered after they marry without their knowledge or consent. You have a right to insist on your own name. If the trouble-maker is a banker, store manager, landlord and/or employer, inform them of your lawful right and suggest they obtain a legal opinion before they deprive you of the right to your own name. You can refer them to the NYCLU and show them this book.

There is a formal procedure for changing ones name which some women choose to go through to regain their maiden names. The advantage of doing this is that if a motor vehicles bureau or voter registration board balks at changing your name on their records, you will have an official legal document to show them.

If you wish to go through a formal name change procedure, you must file a petition in either the county court or supreme court of the county in which you live. You will probably need to consult a lawyer. In New York City the petition may be filed in Supreme Court or any branch of the Civil Court in any county within the city [*Civil Rights Law §§60-64*]. The petition must be in writing, signed, and notarized. It must specify the grounds of the application, your name, date and place of birth, age and residence, and must state whether you have ever been convicted of a crime, adjudicated a bankrupt and whether there are any liens or judgments outstanding against you or legal proceedings to which you are a party. If so, you must explain them. Your birth certificate or a certified transcript of it must be attached. A notice of the proposed change must be published in the newspaper [*Civil Rights Law §61*].

16. REPRODUCTIVE FREEDOM

Birth control

The most effective contraceptives for women (i.e., pills, IUD and diaphragm) may be obtained only with a doctor's prescription from a licensed pharmacist. No private doctor is required to treat any patient if he or she doesn't want to, but if you go to a state or city-run clinic, you have certain rights.

A public clinic may not:

- refuse to prescribe contraceptives for any person because that person is unmarried.
- require a woman to obtain her husband's consent before prescribing contraceptives for her.
- refuse to prescribe contraceptives for an unmarried minor without her parents' consent. The U.S. Supreme Court has declared unconstitutional a New York law prohibiting the sale or distribution of contraceptives to minors under the age of 16. [*Carey v. Population Services International* _____ *U.S.* _____, *52 L.Ed. 2d 675 (1977)*].*

Venereal disease

New York law provides that a minor may be diagnosed and treated for venereal disease without the knowledge or consent of parents or guardians [*Public Health Law §2305 (McKinney 1971)*].

Abortion

Under New York law, the only limitation on the right of a woman to obtain an abortion during the first trimester of pregnancy is that it must be performed by a licensed physician.

During the second trimester, New York law requires abortions to be performed in hospitals on an in-patient basis [*Public Health Law §4164 (McKinney Supp. 1975)*].

During the last trimester (after 24 weeks) a woman may obtain an abortion only if it is necessary to preserve her life or health. [*New York Penal Law §125.05; Roe v. Wade, 410 U.S.*

---

*Reproduced in appendix to Chapter 16.

113 (1973)].

Consent: Married women may not be required by a public clinic to obtain the consent of their husbands for an abortion and a minor may not be required to obtain parental consent for an abortion. [*Planned Parenthood of Central Missouri v. Danforth, 428 U.S. 788 (1976)].**

Refusal of hospitals to perform abortions: The United States Supreme Court has ruled that public hospitals may have a policy of not allowing *elective abortions* to be performed—even if there is a doctor on the staff willing to do them [*Poelker v. Doe* _____ *U.S.* _____, *53 L.Ed. 2d 528 (1977)].*

The Supreme Court did not rule on whether a public hospital may refuse to permit or provide for *medically necessary or therapeutic abortions.* Moreover, the term "medically necessary" has been defined to be a medical decision based on physical and psychological health and including such considerations as familial and age factors. Also, a public hospital may be required to permit abortions under the state constitution or under local laws. If you are refused an abortion in a public hospital, call the New York Civil Liberties Union.

Medicaid for abortions: Although the Supreme Court did rule that states are not required to pay for abortions for poor women, it did not prohibit states from paying these costs. [*Maher v. Roe* _____ *U.S.* _____, *53 L.Ed. 2d 484 (1977); Beal v. Doe* _____ *U.S.* _____, *53 L.Ed. 2d 464 (1977)].* At the time of this publication (August, 1977) New York law provided Medicaid payments for women who could not afford abortions. If you are eligible for Medicaid and have been denied Medicaid payments for an abortion, contact the New York Civil Liberties Union.

Fetal death certificate: New York law requires all physicians performing abortions to fill out a fetal death certificate [*Public Health Law, §§4160—4161 (McKinney 1971)].* This certificate contains the name of the woman on whom the abortion was performed and is registered in the central state computer. The New York City Health Code requires that a woman's name and address appear on a termination of pregnancy certificate which must be filed with the City Department of Health [*N.Y.C. Health Code §204*]. The practice of requiring the physician to include a woman's name and address on the certificate has been upheld by the New York Court of Appeals [*Schulman*

---

*Reproduced in appendix to Chapter 16.

v. New York Health & Hospitals Corp., 38 NY 2d 234 (1975)].
The Supreme Court upheld similar record-keeping requirements in *Danforth* (supra). Your doctor could be prosecuted for refusing to turn over the information to the state, even if you do not consent to his or her doing so.

Sterilization

Restrictions: It is probably true that public hospitals may not refuse to sterilize a patient who requests the procedure [*Hathaway v. Worcester City Hospital, 475 F.2d 701 (1st Cir. 1973), application for stay of mandate denied 411 U.S. 929 (1973)*]. However, since the recent Supreme Court decisions on abortion, the future of this area of law is unclear. If you are refused a sterilization in a public hospital contact NYCLU for assistance.

Consent: A public hospital may not require a woman to obtain her husband's consent before she can be sterilized.

Although parental consent to the sterilization of a minor is not expressly required by law, it is highly unlikely that any public hospital would sterilize a minor without her parents' consent as it might well be liable for damages in a court action.

Involuntary sterilization: Sterilization operations are irreversible and you have an absolute right not to be sterilized against your will. You cannot lose welfare or any other state benefits by refusing to be sterilized no matter whether you are married or how many children you have had [*Public Health Service Act, 42 USC §300a-5 (1974); Relf v. Weinberger, 372 F. Supp. 1196 (DDC 1974)*].

Regulations and waiting periods: *Outside New York City;*
1. Only sterilizations covered by Medicaid are subject to regulations;
2. The patient must be over 21;
3. There is a 72-hour waiting period for non-emergency sterilizations after you give your written consent;
4. You must be provided with a full explanation of the procedure and the risks;

In New York City: All sterilizations performed in New York City are subject to Chapter 22 Title C of the Administrative Code which provides:
1. The patient must be over 21.

2. There must be a 30-day waiting period after the patient signs consent unless she is admitted to a hospital for childbirth or emergency abdominal surgery unexpectedly and before the 30-day period has passed.

3. No consent may be signed while a woman is in the hospital for childbirth or abortion.

Medicaid

If you are on Medicaid, the State of New York does provide free of charge a wide range of family planning services, including contraceptives, abortion and sterilization [*Social Services Law §§131-(3), 365-a, subd. 3(c), (McKinney 1976)*]. This applies to sexually active women under 21 years old as well.

Resources

For information on family planning and for medical services including abortion and sterilization and prescription of contraceptives, call your local Planned Parenthood chapter. The national office is at 810 Seventh Avenue, New York, NY 10019, (212) 541-7800. They can refer you to your local office. The New York City office is at 300 Park Avenue South, New York, NY 10010, telephone (212) 677-3040.

References

For information on abortion techniques, contraception and a list of Planned Parenthood offices, see: Planned Parenthood of New York City *Abortion: A Woman's Guide,* N.Y.: Abelard-Schuman Ltd., 1973 (paperback $2.95).

17. RAPE

Under New York law, rapists are defined by statute as male and rape victims as female. (Other types of sexual assaults on males and by females are prohibited under different sections of the penal law.)

There are three degrees of rape, defined as follows:

Rape in the First Degree.

A male is guilty of rape in the first degree when he engages in sexual intercourse with a female:

1. By forcible compulsion; or
2. Who is incapable of consent by reason of being physically helpless; or
3. Who is less than 11 years old [*Penal Law §130.35 (McKinney 1975)*]

Rape in the Second Degree

A male is guilty of rape in the second degree when, being 18 years old or more, he engages in sexual intercourse with a female less than 14 years old [*Penal Law §130.30 (McKinney 1975)*].

Rape in the Third Degree

A male is guilty of rape in the third degree when:

1. He engages in sexual intercourse with a female who is incapable of consent by reason of some factor other than being less than 17 years old; or
2. Being twenty-one years old or more, he engages in sexual intercourse with a female less than 17 years old [*Penal Law §130.25 (McKinney 1975)*].

Rape by husband

Under New York law, the word "female" when used in the rape statute means "any female person who is not married to the actor" [*Penal Law §130.00 (4) (McKinney 1975)*]. Thus, it is not a crime for a husband to rape his wife himself (although he can be prosecuted for aiding another man to rape her).

Corroboration

New York law no longer requires that every element of the crime of rape (lack of consent, penetration, and rapist's identity) be corroborated by independent evidence, other than the victim's testimony, before a jury will be allowed to consider the case [*Penal Law §130.16*]. The only exception is where the alleged victim is deemed by law to be incapable of consenting to the act because she is under 17 years old or is mentally defective or incapacitated, in which case corroboration is still required [*Penal Law §130.16, McKinney 1975*]. Thus, a defendant charged with forcible rape may be prosecuted and convicted solely on the testimony of the rape victim, just as he could be if charged with any other crime.

What to do if you are raped

Although corroboration is no longer legally required before a rape case can go to a jury, obviously you will have a far better chance of successfully prosecuting a rapist if you have evidence besides your own testimony that you were raped. Therefore, even though it is hard to think about a future criminal prosecution just after having been raped, it is important to take certain practical steps immediately.

1) *Call the police.* Many police departments these days have specially trained rape squads, usually consisting of female officers. Even if no rape squad exists in your city, if you would feel more comfortable talking to another woman, you should certainly ask to do so.

2) *Tell a friend or neighbor* what happened to you right away and show that person any injuries you have suffered so that you have a witness to your mental and physical condition immediately after the attack. Even though many women are too terrified to do anything at all after having been raped, a victim's delay in reporting the crime is often used by defense lawyers to try to show that a woman was not raped at all but simply made up a story later because she felt guilty or was angry at the man.

3) *Don't bathe or douche* before you see the police. Even though that may be what you most want to do, it is important not to wash away evidence of sexual emission.

4) *Save your underclothes* and any clothing torn or soiled during the rape. This will be evidence that the rapist used force. These should be given to the police investigator. Similarly, you should not straighten up any signs of a struggle in your home before police arrive.

5) *Go to a hospital* or have the police take you to one. The doctor should note the presence of injuries and make slides to detect the presence of semen. The medical record and evidence collected by the doctor may not be given to anyone without your consent. If you think there is a chance that you may become pregnant, talk to the doctor about the advisability of taking a "morning-after pill" to prevent conception, or consult your own doctor immediately. You should also have a VD test.

Prosecuting the rapist

Many women simply never report rapes or fail to prosecute rapists because they find the process painful and humiliating and would rather forget the whole thing. This is understandable, but it also keeps rapists on the street. If you decide you want to prosecute, you should be prepared to:

1) talk to the police more than once;

2) go to the police station several times to identify photographs or persons in a line-up;

3) talk to the District Attorney;

4) testify and undergo cross-examination in court in the presence of the person you have accused (who has a constitutional right to confront his accuser).

Victim's cross-examination

One of the most unpleasant parts of any rape prosecution for the victim has traditionally been cross-examination by the defense attorney concerning her sex life. The New York law, however, now limits the defendant's right to introduce evidence of the victim's past sexual conduct except in certain instances where it is directly relevant to the case [*NY CPL §60.42 (McKinney Supp. 1975)*]. The law now provides:

Evidence of a victim's sexual conduct shall not be admissible in a prosecution for [rape] unless such evidence:

1) proves or tends to prove specific instances of the victim's prior sexual conduct with the accused; or

2) proves or tends to prove that the victim has been convicted of an offense under section 230.00 of the penal law [prostitution] within three years prior to the sex offense which is the subject of the prosecution; or

3) rebuts evidence introduced by the people of the victim's failure to engage in sexual intercourse, deviate sexual intercourse or sexual contact during a given period of time; or

4) rebuts evidence introduced by the people which proves or tends to prove that the accused is the cause of pregnancy or disease of the victim, or the source of semen found in the victim;

5) is determined by the court after an offer of proof by the accused outside the hearing of the jury, or such hearing as the court may require, and a statement by the court of its findings of fact essential to its determination, to be relevant and admissible in the interests of justice [*Added L.1975, c. 230, §1*]

Compensation

You may be entitled to be reimbursed by the New York State Crime Victim's Compensation Board for medical and psychiatric expenses of over $100 incurred as a result of the rape, and back pay for time over two weeks lost from work because of the rape. To be eligible for compensation you must report the rape to the police within 48 hours.

The Board will send you the form to be filed if you write or call:

Crime Victims Compensation Board
875 Central Avenue
Albany, New York 12206
(518) 457-4060
or
270 Broadway
New York, New York 10007
(212) 488-5080

18. ASSAULT

Assault by a family member

A woman whose husband (or other family member) has assaulted or attempted or threatened to assault her or her children or other members of the family, or has acted in a disorderly, harassing, menacing or recklessly dangerous manner, has two legal remedies [§812 *Family Court Act (McKinney 1977)*].

1) Family Court: Family Court judges have the power in cases involving violence among family members to issue an Order of Protection to a person who petitions for one [§821 *et. seq. Family Court Act (McKinney 1975)*]. This order may provide that the person complained of must:

a) stay away from the woman/children (only in extreme cases);

b) stop the behavior complained of;

c) give proper attention to care of the home;

d) refrain from acts which make the home not a proper place for a child;

e) visit the child only at stated periods [*Family Court Act §842 (McKinney 1975)*].

The Family Court judge has the power to issue the Order of Protection for a period of up to one year. The punishment for disobeying it may be imprisonment for up to six months but this penalty is rarely applied [*Family Court Act §846 (McKinney 1975)*].

2) Criminal Court: If a woman chooses to proceed in criminal court, her relative will be treated like any other criminal defendant. He may be arrested and bail may be set; he may be tried or plead guilty and may be sentenced to prison. Only persons over eighteen may be prosecuted in criminal court; all cases involving minors are heard in family court.

Which remedy to pursue

Which remedy to pursue depends on various factors. In serious cases, criminal court may be the only solution. In less serious cases, where a woman feels that her husband or other relative may be deterred from committing further acts of violence by less serious action than a criminal prosecution, she may prefer to proceed in a family court. It should be noted that the law permitting disputes involving family violence to be heard in criminal court is very new and thus there has been no experience yet to show how the criminal court will deal with family violence. A decision to go to one court or the other is final. You cannot switch if you don't like what is happening in the forum you have chosen. If you decide to go to criminal court, remember that, as with all other criminal complaints, the district attorney has the final discretion to decide whether to charge anyone with a crime.

Procedure

A woman who wants an Order of Protection should simply go to court to ask for it. The exact procedure for getting the order may vary somewhat from place to place, so you should ask at your local family court precisely what to do.

The court may order the probation service to interview you concerning the advisability of petitioning for a protective order and they may attempt to have you and your husband go through conciliation proceedings and attempt to reach an informal agreement. If the probation interviewer thinks you and your husband should agree informally but you prefer to petition the court for a formal order, you may not be prevented from doing so, nor can probation compel you or your husband to appear at any conference to do anything else. Probation services are purely voluntary [*Family Court Act, §823 (McKinney 1975)*].

If you decide to petition for an order, the court may issue a summons requiring your husband to appear in court and a hearing will be held [*Family Court Act, §825 (McKinney 1975)*]. If he cannot be found or refuses to appear, or appears likely to run away or continues to endanger your safety, the court can issue a warrant for his arrest [*Family Court Act, §827 (McKinney 1975)*]. Pending the hearing, the court may issue a temporary order of protection.

Attorneys

You have a right to have an attorney at the hearing, but the court will not provide you with one free of charge if you cannot afford one.

Criminal court

If you choose a criminal prosecution you should go to the criminal court and ask where to go to file a complaint. You will be interviewed by an assistant district attorney who may write up a complaint and inform you of a date to appear in court to testify. You do not need an attorney.

Assault by a non-family member

If you or your children are assaulted by a man you are living with but are not married to and have no children with, you must follow the same procedure you would use if you were assaulted by a stranger: call the police. If the police won't help, you should go to criminal court and ask to have a District Attorney draw up a criminal complaint. The man may be arrested and brought to court just like any other criminal assailant.

Reference

"A Handbook for Beaten Women" (free)
South Brooklyn Legal Services
152 Court Street
Brooklyn, N.Y. 12201

19. Offices of the New York Civil Liberties Union

Main Office
84 Fifth Avenue
New York, N.Y. 10011
(212) 924-7800

Central New York Chapter
713 Wilson Building
310 South Salina Street
Syracuse, N.Y. 13202
(315) 471-2821

Niagara Frontier Chapter
303 Crosby Building
170 Franklin Street
Buffalo, N.Y. 14202
(716) 855-1493

Genesee Valley Chapter
429 Powers Building
Rochester, N.Y. 14614
(716) 454-4334

Suffolk County Chapter
First United Methodist Church
58 Wheeler Road
Central Islip, N.Y. 11722
(516) 234-6676

Nassau County Chapter
210 Old Country Road
Mineola, N.Y. 11501
(516) 741-8520

Westchester County Chapter
400 Tarrytown Road
Greenburgh, N.Y. 10607
(914) 946-5127

The New York Civil Liberties Union also has chapters in Brooklyn, Rockland County, Mid Hudson area, Albany and Ithaca. For information about whom to contact in those chapters, write or call the main office of the NYCLU.

APPENDIX A
Chapter 3 (Employment)

**Equal Employment Opportunity Commission
Guidelines on Discrimination Because of Sex,
29 C.F.R. §1604.1—1604.10**

§1604.1   General principles.

(a) References to "employer" or "employers" in this Part 1604
state principles that are applicable not only to employers but also to
labor organizations and to employment agencies insofar as their action or inaction may adversely affect employment opportunities.

(b) To the extent that the views expressed in prior Commission
pronouncements are inconsistent with the views expressed herein,
such prior views are hereby overruled.

(c) The Commission will continue to consider particular problems relating to sex discrimination on a case-by-case basis.

§1604.2   Sex as a bona fide occupational qualification.

(a) The commission believes that the bona fide occupational
qualification exception as to sex should be interpreted narrowly.
Labels—"Men's jobs" and "Women's jobs"—tend to deny
employment opportunities unnecessarily to one sex or the other.

(1) The Commission will find that the following situations do not
warrant the application of the bona fide occupational qualification
exception:

(i) The refusal to hire a woman because of her sex based on
assumptions of the comparative employment characteristics of wom-
en in general. For example, the assumption that the turnover rate
among women is higher than among men.

(ii) The refusal to hire an individual based on stereotyped char-
acterizations of the sexes. Such stereotypes include, for example, that
men are less capable of assembling intricate equipment; that women
are less capable of aggressive salesmanship. The principle of non-
discrimination requires that individuals be considered on the basis of
individual capacities and not on the basis of any characteristics generally attributed to the group.

(iii) The refusal to hire an individual because of the preferences of coworkers, the employer, clients or customers except as covered specifically in paragraph (a)(2) of this section.

(2) Where it is necessary for the purpose of authenticity or genuineness, the Commission will consider sex to be a bona fide occupational qualification, e.g., an actor or actress.

(b) Effect of sex-oriented State employment legislation.

(1) Many States have enacted laws or promulgated administrative regulations with respect to the employment of females. Among these laws are those which prohibit or limit the employment of females, e.g., the employment of females in certain occupations, in jobs requiring the lifting or carrying of weights exceeding certain prescribed limits, during certain hours of the night, for more than a specified number of hours per day or per week, and for certain periods of time before and after childbirth. The Commission has found that such laws and regulations do not take into account the capacities, preferences, and abilities of individual females and, therefore, discriminate on the basis of sex. The Commission has concluded that such laws and regulations conflict with and are superseded by title VII of the Civil Rights Act of 1964. Accordingly, such laws will not be considered a defense to an otherwise established unlawful employment practice or as a basis for the application of the bona fide occupational qualification exception.

(2) The Commission has concluded that State laws and regulations which discriminate on the basis of sex with regard to the employment of minors are in conflict with and are superseded by title VII to the extent that such laws are more restrictive for one sex. Accordingly, restrictions on the employment of minors of one sex over and above those imposed on minors of the other sex will not be considered a defense to an otherwise established unlawful employment practice or as a basis for the application of the bona fide occupational qualification exception.

(3) A number of States require that minimum wage and premium pay for overtime be provided for female employees. An employer will be deemed to have engaged in an unlawful employment practice if:

(i) It refuses to hire or otherwise adversely affects the employment opportunities of female applicants or employees in order to avoid the payment of minimum wages or overtime pay required by State law; or

(ii) It does not provide the same benefits for male employees.

(4) As to other kinds of sex-oriented State employment laws, such as those requiring special rest and meal periods or physical facilities for women, provision of these benefits to one sex only will be a violation of title VII. An employer will be deemed to have engaged in an unlawful employment practice if:

(i) It refuses to hire or otherwise adversely affects the employment opportunities of female applicants or employees in order to avoid the provision of such benefits; or

(ii) It does not provide the same benefits for male employees. If the employer can prove that business necessity precludes providing these benefits to both men and women, then the State law is in conflict with and superseded by title VII as to this employer. In this situation, the employer shall not provide such benefits to members of either sex.

(5) Some States require that separate restrooms be provided for employees of each sex. An employer will be deemed to have engaged in an unlawful employment practice if it refuses to hire or otherwise adversely affects the employment opportunities of applicants or employees in order to avoid the provision of such restrooms for persons of that sex.

§1604.3 Separate lines of progression and seniority systems.

(a) It is an unlawful employment practice to classify a job as "male" or "female" or to maintain separate lines of progression or separate seniority lists based on sex where this would adversely affect any employee unless sex is a bona fide occupational qualification for that job. Accordingly, employment practices are unlawful which arbitrarily classify jobs so that:

(1) A female is prohibited from applying for a job labeled "male," or for a job in a "male" line of progression; and vice versa.

(2) A male scheduled for layoff is prohibited from displacing a less senior female on a "female" seniority list; and vice versa.

(b) A Seniority system or line of progression which distinguishes between "light" and "heavy" jobs constitutes an unlawful employment practice if it operates as a disguised form of classification by sex, or creates unreasonable obstacles to the advancement by members of either sex into jobs which members of that sex would reasonably be expected to perform.

§1604.4 Discrimination against married women.

(a) The Commission has determined that an employer's rule which forbids or restricts the employment of married women and which is not applicable to married men is a discrimination based on sex prohibited by title VII of the Civil Rights Act. It does not seem to us relevant that the rule is not directed against all females, but only against married females, for so long as sex is a factor in the application of the rule, such application involves a discrimination based on sex.

(b) It may be that under certain circumstances, such a rule could be justified within the meaning of section 703(e)(1) of title VII. We express no opinion on this question at this time except to point out that sex as a bona fide occupational qualification must be justified in terms of the peculiar requirements of the particular job and not on the basis of a general principle such as the desirability of spreading work.

§1604.5   Job opportunities advertising.

It is a violation of title VII for a help-wanted advertisement to indicate a preference, limitation, specification, or discrimination based on sex unless sex is a bona fide occupational qualification for the particular job involved. The placement of an advertisement in columns classified by publishers on the basis of sex, such as columns headed "Male" or "Female," will be considered an expression of a preference, limitation, specification, or discrimination based on sex.

§1604.6   Employment agencies.

(a) Section 703(b) of the Civil Rights Act specifically states that it shall be unlawful for an employment agency to discriminate against any individual because of sex. The Commission has determined that private employment agencies which deal exclusively with one sex are engaged in an unlawful employment practice, except to the extent that such agencies limit their services to furnishing employees for particular jobs for which sex is a bona fide occupational qualification.

(b) An employment agency that receives a job order containing an unlawful sex specification will share responsibility with the employer placing the job order if the agency fills the order knowing that the sex specification is not based upon a bona fide occupational qualification. However, an employment agency will not be deemed to be in violation of the law, regardless of the determination as to the employer, if the agency does not have reason to believe that the employer's claim of bona fide occupational qualification is without substance and the agency makes and maintains a written record available to the Commission of each such job order. Such record shall include the name of the employer, the description of the job and the basis for the employer's claim of bona fide occupational qualification.

(c) It is the responsibility of employment agencies to keep informed of opinions and decisions of the Commission on sex discrimination.

§1604.7   Pre-employment inquiries as to sex.

A pre-employment inquiry may ask "Male......., Female......."; or "Mr. Mrs. Miss," provided that the inquiry is made in good faith for a nondiscriminatory purpose. Any pre-employment inquiry in connection with prospective employment which expresses directly or indirectly any limitation, specification, or discrimination as to sex shall be unlawful unless based upon a bona fide occupational qualification.

§1604.8   Relationship of title VII to the Equal Pay Act.

(a) The employee coverage of the prohibitions against discrimination based on sex contained in title VII is coextensive with that of the other prohibitions contained in title VII and is not limited by section 703(h) to those employees covered by the Fair Labor Standards Act.

(b) By virtue of section 703(h), a defense based on the Equal Pay Act may be raised in a proceeding under title VII.

(c) Where such a defense is raised the Commission will give appropriate consideration to the interpretations of the Administrator, Wage and Hour Division, Department of Labor, but will not be bound thereby.

§1604.9 Fringe benefits.

(a) "Fringe benefits," as used herein, includes medical, hospital, accident, life insurance and retirement benefits; profit-sharing and bonus plans; leave; and other terms, conditions, and privileges of employment.

(b) It shall be an unlawful employment practice for an employer to discriminate between men and women with regard to fringe benefits.

(c) Where an employer conditions benefits available to employees and their spouses and families on whether the employee is the "head of the household" or "principal wage earner" in the family unit, the benefits tend to be available only to male employees and their families. Due to the fact that such conditioning discriminatorily affects the rights of women employees, and that "head of household" or "principal wage earner" status bears no relationship to job performance, benefits which are so conditioned will be found a prima facie violation of the prohibitions against sex discrimination contained in the act.

(d) It shall be an unlawful employment practice for an employer to make available benefits for the wives and families of male employees where the same benefits are not made available for the husbands and families of female employees; or to make available benefits for the wives of male employees which are not made available for female employees; or to make available benefits to the husbands of female employees which are not made available for male employees. An example of such an unlawful employment practice is a situation in which wives of male employees receive maternity benefits while female employees receive no such benefits.

(e) It shall not be a defense under title VII to a charge of sex discrimination in benefits that the cost of such benefits is greater with respect to one sex than the other.

(f) It shall be an unlawful employment practice for an employer to have a pension or retirement plan which establishes different optional or compulsory retirement ages based on sex, or which differentiates in benefits on the basis of sex. A statement of the General Counsel of September 13, 1968, providing for a phasing out of differentials with regard to optional retirement age for certain incumbent employees is hereby withdrawn.

§1604.10 Employment policies relating to pregnancy and childbirth.

(a) A written or unwritten employment policy or practice which excludes from employment applicants or employees because of pregnancy is in prima facie violation of title VII.

(b) Disabilities caused or contributed to by pregnancy, miscarriage, abortion, childbirth, and recovery therefrom are, for all job-related purposes, temporary disabilities and should be treated as such under any health or temporary disability insurance or sick leave plan available in connection with employment. Written and unwritten employment policies and practices involving matters such as the commencement and duration of leave, the availability of extensions, the accrual of seniority and other benefits and privileges, reinstatement, and payment under any health or temporary disability insurance or sick leave plan, formal or informal, shall be applied to disability due to pregnancy or childbirth on the same terms and conditions as they are applied to other temporary disabilities.

(c) Where the termination of an employee who is temporarily disabled is caused by an employment policy under which insufficient or no leave is available, such a termination violates the act if it has a disparate impact on employees of one sex and is not justified by business necessity.

Diaz v. Pan American World Airways, Inc., 442 F.2d 385 (5th Cir.) *cert. denied* 404 U.S. 950 (1971)

Pan Am admitted that it had a policy of restricting its hiring for the cabin attendant position to females. Thus, both parties stipulated that the primary issue for the District Court was whether, for the job of flight cabin attendant, being a female is a "bona fide occupational qualification (hereafter BFOQ) reasonably necessary to the normal operation" of Pan American's business. . . .

We begin with the proposition that the use of the word "necessary" in section 703(e) requires that we apply a business *necessity* test, not a business *convenience* test. That is to say, discrimination based on sex is valid only when the *essence* of the business operation would be undermined by not hiring members of one sex exclusively.

The primary function of an airline is to transport passengers safely from one point to another. While a pleasant environment, enhanced by the obvious cosmetic effect that female stewardesses provide as well as, according to the finding of the trial court, their apparent ability to perform the non-mechanical functions of the job in a more effective manner than most men, may all be important, they are tangential to the essence of the business involved. No one has suggested that having male stewards will so seriously affect the operation of an airline as to jeopardize or even minimize its ability to provide safe transportation from one place to another. Indeed the record discloses that many airlines including Pan Am have utilized both men and women flight cabin attendants in the past and Pan Am, even at the time of this suit, has 283 male stewards employed on some of its foreign flights.

. . . We do not mean to imply, of course, that Pan Am cannot take into consideration the ability of *individuals* to perform the non-mechanical functions of the job. What we hold is that because the non-mechanical aspects of the job of flight cabin attendant are not "reasonably necessary to the normal operation" of Pan Am's business, Pan Am cannot exclude *all* males simply because *most* males may not perform adequately. . . .

Similarly, we do not feel that the fact that Pan Am's passengers prefer female stewardesses should alter our judgment. On this subject, EEOC guidelines state that a BFOQ ought not be based on "the refusal to hire an individual because of preferences of co-workers, the employer, clients or customers . . . ."

. . . While we recognize that the public's expectation of finding one sex in a particular role may cause some initial difficulty, it would be totally anomalous if we were to allow the preferences and prejudices of the customers to determine whether the sex discrimination was valid. Indeed, it was, to a large extent, these very prejudices the Act was meant to overcome. Thus, we feel that customer preference may be taken into account only when it is based on the company's inability to perform the primary function or service it offers.

Of course, Pan Am argues that the customers' preferences are not based on "stereotyped thinking," but the ability of women stewardesses to better provide the non-mechanical aspects of the job. Again, as stated above, since these aspects are tangential to the business, the fact that customers prefer them cannot justify sex discrimination.

Phillips v. Martin Marietta Corp. 400 U.S. 542 (1971)

Per Curiam.

Petitioner Mrs. Ida Phillips commenced an action in the United States District Court for the Middle District of Florida under Title VII of the Civil Rights Act of 1964 alleging that she had been denied employment because of her sex. The District Court granted summary judgment for Martin Marietta Corp. (Martin) on the basis of the following showing: (1) in 1966 Martin informed Mrs. Phillips that it was not accepting job applications from women with pre-school-age children;

(2) as of the time of the motion for summary judgment, Martin employed men with pre-school-age children; (3) at the time Mrs. Phillips applied, 70-75% of the applicants for the position she sought were women; 75-80% of those hired for the position, assembly trainee, were women, hence no question of bias against women as such was presented.

The Court of Appeals for the Fifth Circuit affirmed, 411 F2d 1, and denied a rehearing en banc. . . .

Section 703(a) of the Civil Rights Act of 1964 requires that persons of like qualifications be given employment opportunities irrespective of their sex. The Court of Appeals therefore erred in reading this section as permitting one hiring policy for women and another for men—each having pre-school-age children. The existence of such conflicting family obligations, if demonstrably more relevant to job performance for a woman than for a man, could arguably be a basis for distinction under §703(e) of the Act. But that is a matter of evidence tending to show that the condition in question "is a bona fide occupational qualification reasonably necessary to the normal operation of that particular business or enterprise." The record before us, however, is not adequate for resolution of these important issues . . . . Summary judgment was therefore improper and we remand for fuller development of the record and for further consideration.

Vacated and remanded.

The company, of course, could not show that their rule was justified and the case was finally settled out of court.

Dothard v. Rawlinson, _____ U.S. _____, 53 L.Ed. 2d 786 (1977)

Mr. Justice Stewart delivered the opinion of the Court.

The appellee, Dianne Rawlinson, sought employment with the Alabama Board of Corrections as a prison guard, called in Alabama a "correctional counselor." After her application was rejected, she brought this class suit under Title VII of the Civil Rights Act of 1964, . . . alleging that she had been denied employment because of her sex in violation of federal law. A three-judge Federal District Court for the Middle District of Alabama decided in her favor. . . .

I

At the time she applied for a position as correctional counselor trainee, Rawlinson was a 22-year-old college graduate whose major course of study had been correctional psychology. She was refused employment because she failed to meet the minimum 120-pound weight requirement established by an Alabama statute. The statute also establishes a height minimum of 5 feet and 2 inches (footnote omitted).

After her application was rejected because of her weight, Rawlinson filed a charge with the Equal Employment Opportunity Commission, and ultimately received a right to sue letter (footnote omitted). She then filed a complaint in the District Court on behalf of herself and other similarly situated women, challenging the statutory height and weight minima as violative of Title VII and the Equal Protection Clause of the Fourteenth Amendment (footnote omitted). . . . While the suit was pending, the Alabama Board of Corrections adopted Administrative Regulation 204, establishing gender criteria for assigning correctional counselors to maximum security institutions for "contact positions," that is, positions requiring continual close physical proximity to inmates of the institution (footnote omitted). Rawlinson amended her class-action complaint by adding a challenge to Regulation 204 as also violative of Title VII and the Fourteenth Amendment.

Like most correctional facilities in the United States (footnote omitted), Alabama's prisons are segregated on the basis of sex. Currently the Alabama Board of Corrections operates four major all-male penitentiaries . . . .

A correctional counselor's primary duty within these institutions is to maintain security and control of the inmates by continually supervising and observing their activities (footnote omitted). . . .

At the time this litigation was in the District Court, the Board of Corrections employed a total of 435 people in various correctional counselor positions, 56 of whom were women. Of those 56 women, 21 were employed at the Julia Tutwiler Prison for Women, 13 were employed in noncontact positions at the four male maximum security institutions, and the remaining 22 were employed at the other institutions operated by the Alabama Board of Corrections. Because most of Alabama's prisoners are held at the four maximum security male penitentiaries, 336 of the 435 correctional counselor jobs were in those institutions, a majority of them concededly in the "contact" classification (footnote omitted). Thus, even though meeting the statutory height and weight requirements, women applicants could under Regulation 204 compete equally with men for only about 25% of the correctional counselor jobs available in the Alabama prison system.

II

In enacting Title VII, Congress required "the removal of artificial, arbitrary, and unnecessary barriers to employment when the barriers operate invidiously to discriminate on the basis of racial or other impermissible classification." . . . The District Court found that the minimum statutory height and weight requirements that applicants for employment as correctional counselors must meet constitute the sort of arbitrary barrier to equal employment opportunity that Title VII forbids (footnote omitted). The appellants assert that the District Court erred both in finding that the height and weight standards discriminate against women, and in its refusal to find that, even if they do, these standards are justified as "job related."

The gist of the claim that the statutory height and weight requirements discriminate against women does not involve an assertion of purposeful discriminatory motive (footnote omitted). It is asserted, rather, that these facially neutral qualification standards work in fact disproportionately to exclude women from eligibility for employment by the Alabama Board of Corrections. . . .

. . . [T]o establish a prima facie case of discrimination, a plaintiff need only show that the facially neutral standards in question select applicants for hire in a significantly discriminatory pattern. Once it is thus shown that the employment standards are discriminatory in effect, the employer must meet "the burden of showing that any given requirement [has]. . . a manifest relation to the employment in question." . . . If the employer proves that the challenged requirements are job related, the plaintiff may then show that other selection devices without a similar discriminatory effect would also "serve the employer's legitimate interest in 'efficient and trustworthy workmanship.' " . . .

Although women 14 years of age or older comprise 52.75% of the Alabama population and 36.89% of its total labor force, they hold only 12.9% of its correctional counselor positions. In considering the effect of the minimum height and weight standards on this disparity in rate of hiring between the sexes, the District Court found that the 5'2" requirement would operate to exclude 33.29% of the women in the United States between the ages of 18-79, while excluding only 1.28% of men between the same ages. The 120-pound weight restriction would exclude 22.29% of the women and 2.35% of the men in this age group. When the height and weight restrictions are combined, Alabama's statutory standards would exclude 41.13% of the female population while excluding less than one percent of the male population (footnote omitted). Accordingly, the District Court found that Rawlinson had made out a prima facie case of unlawful sex discrimination. . . .

We turn . . . to the appellants' argument that they have rebutted the prima facie case of discrimination by showing that the height and weight requirements are job related. These requirements, they say, have a relationship to strength, a sufficient but unspecified amount of which is essential to effective job performance as a correctional counselor. In the District Court, however, the appellants produced no evidence correlating the height and weight requirements with the requisite amount of strength thought essential to good job performance. Indeed, they failed to offer evidence of any kind in specific justification of the statutory standards (footnote omitted).

If the job-related quality that the appellants identify is bona fide, their purpose could be achieved by adopting and validating a test for applicants that measures strength directly (footnote omitted). Such a test, fairly administered, would fully satisfy the standards of Title VII because it would be one that "measure[s] the person for the job and not the person in the abstract." . . . But nothing in the present record even approaches such a measurement.

For the reasons we have discussed, the District Court was not in error in holding that Title VII of the Civil Rights Act of 1964, as amended, prohibits application of the statutory height and weight requirements to Rawlinson and the class she represents.

III

Unlike the statutory height and weight requirements, Regulation 204 explicitly discriminates against women on the basis of their sex (footnote omitted). In defense of this overt discrimination, the appellants rely on §703(e) of Title VII, which permits sex-based discrimination "in those certain instances where . . . sex . . . is a bona fide occupational qualification reasonably necessary to the normal operation of that particular business or enterprise."

The District Court rejected the bona fide occupational qualification (bfoq) defense, relying on the virtually uniform view of the federal courts that §703(e) provides only the narrowest of exceptions to the general rule requiring equality of employment opportunities. . . .

We are persuaded—by the restrictive language of §703(e), the relevant legislative history (footnote omitted), and the consistent interpretation of the Equal Employment Opportunity Commission (footnote omitted)—that the bfoq exception was in fact meant to be an extremely narrow exception to the general prohibition of discrimination on the basis of sex (footnote omitted). In the particular factual circumstances of this case, however, we conclude that the District Court erred in rejecting the State's contention that Regulation 204 falls within the narrow ambit of the bfoq exception.

The environment in Alabama's penitentiaries is a peculiarly inhospitable one for human beings of whatever sex. Indeed, a federal district court has held that the conditions of confinement in the prisons of the State, characterized by "rampant violence" and a "jungle atmosphere," are constitutionally intolerable. . . . The record in the present case shows that because of inadequate staff and facilities, no attempt is made in the four maximum security male penitentiaries to classify or segregate inmates according to their offense or level of dangerousness—a procedure that, according to expert testimony, is essential to effective penological administration. Consequently, the estimated 20% of the male prisoners who are sex offenders are scattered throughout the penitentiaries' dormitory facilities.

In this environment of violence and disorganization, it would be an oversimplification to characterize Regulation 204 as an exercise in "romantic paternalism." . . . In the usual case, the argument that a particular job is too dangerous for women may appropriately be met by the rejoinder that it is the purpose of Title VII to allow the individual woman to make that choice for herself (footnote omitted). More is at stake in this case, however, than an individual woman's decision to weigh and accept the risks of employment in a "contact" position in a maximum security male prison.

The essence of a correctional counselor's job is to maintain prison security. A woman's relative ability to maintain order in a male, maximum security, unclassified penitentiary of the type Alabama now runs could be directly reduced by her womanhood. There is a basis in fact for expecting that sex offenders who have criminally assaulted women in the past would be moved to do so again if access to women were established within the prison. There would also be a real risk that other inmates, deprived of a normal heterosexual environment, would assault women guards because they were women (footnote omitted). In a prison system where violence is the order of the day, where inmate access to guards is facilitated by dormitory living arrangements, where every institution is understaffed, and where a substantial portion of the inmate population is composed of sex offenders mixed at random with other prisoners, there are few visible deterrents to inmate assaults on women custodians.

The plaintiffs' own expert testified that dormitory housing for aggressive inmates poses a greater security problem than single-cell lockups, and further testified that it would be unwise to use women as guards in a prison where even 10% of the inmates had been convicted of sex crimes and were not segregated from the other prisoners (footnote omitted). The likelihood that inmates would assault a woman because she was a women would pose a real threat not only to the victim of the assault but also to the basic control of the penitentiary and protection of its inmates and the other security personnel. The employee's very womanhood would thus directly undermine her capacity to provide the security that is the essence of a correctional counselor's responsibility.

There was substantial testimony from experts on both sides of this litigation that the use of women as guards in "contact" positions under the existing conditions in Alabama maximum security male penitentiaries would pose a substantial security problem, directly linked to the sex of the prison guard. On the basis of that evidence, we conclude that the District Court was in error in ruling that being male is not a bona fide occupational qualification for the job of correctional counselor in a "contact" position in an Alabama male maximum security penitentiary (footnote omitted).

The judgment is accordingly affirmed in part and reversed in part, and the case is remanded to the District Court for further proceedings consistent with this opinion.

It is so ordered.

Cleveland Board of Education v. LaFleur
414 U.S. 632 (1974)

Mr. Justice Stewart delivered the opinion of the Court.

The respondents...and the petitioner [in these cases] are female public school teachers. During the 1970-1971 school year, each informed her local school board that she was pregnant; each was compelled by a mandatory maternity leave rule to quit her job without pay several months before the expected birth of her child. These cases call upon us to decide the constitutionality of the school boards' rules.

I

Jo Carol LaFleur and Ann Elizabeth Nelson...are junior high school teachers employed by the Board of Education of Cleveland, Ohio. Pursuant to a rule first adopted in 1952, the school board requires every pregnant school teacher to take maternity leave without pay, beginning five months before the expected birth of her child. Application for such leave must be made no later than two weeks prior to the date of departure. A teacher on maternity leave is not allowed to return to work until the beginning of the next regular school semester which follows the date when her child attains the age of three months. A doctor's certificate attesting to the health of the teacher is a prerequisite to return; an additional physical examination may be required. The teacher on maternity leave is not promised re-employment after the birth of the child; she is merely given priority in reassignment to a position for which she is qualified. Failure to comply with the mandatory maternity leave provisions is ground for dismissal (footnote omitted).

Neither Mrs. LaFleur nor Mrs. Nelson wished to take an unpaid maternity leave; each wanted to continue teaching until the end of the school year (footnote omitted). Because of the mandatory maternity leave rule, however, each was required to leave her job in March 1971 (footnote omitted). The two women then filed separate suits...challenging the constitutionality of the maternity leave rule. The District Court tried the cases together, and rejected the plaintiffs' arguments. 326 F Supp 1208. A divided panel of the United States Court of Appeals for the Sixth Circuit reversed, finding the Cleveland rule in violation of the Equal Protection Clause of the Fourteenth Amendment (footnote omitted). 465 F2d 1184.

. . .Susan Cohen was employed by the School Board of Chesterfield County, Virginia. That school board's maternity leave regulation requires that a pregnant teacher leave work at least four months prior to the expected birth of her child. Notice in writing must be given to the school board at least six months prior to the expected birth date. A teacher on maternity leave is declared re-eligible for employment when she submits written notice from a physician that she is physically fit for re-employment, and when she can give assurance that care of the child will cause only minimal interference with her job responsibilities. The teacher is guaranteed re-employment no later than the first day of the school year following the date upon which she is declared re-eligible (footnote omitted).

Mrs. Cohen informed the Chesterfield County School Board in November 1970, that she was pregnant and expected the birth of her child about April 28, 1971 (footnote omitted). She initially requested that she be permitted to continue teaching until April 1, 1971 (footnote omitted). The school board rejected the request, as it did Mrs. Cohen's subsequent suggestion that she be allowed to teach until January 21, 1971, the end of the first school semester. Instead, she was required to leave her teaching job on December 18, 1970. She subsequently filed this suit. . . . The District Court held that the school board regulation violates the Equal Protection Clause, and granted an appropriate relief. 326 F Supp 1159. A divided panel of the Fourth Circuit affirmed, but, on rehearing en banc, the Court of Appeals upheld the constitutionality of the challenged regulation in a 4-3 decision. 474 F2nd 395.

We granted certiorari in both cases. . . in order to resolve the conflict between the Court of Appeals regarding the constitutionality of such mandatory maternity leave rules for public school teachers (footnote omitted).

II

This Court has long recognized that freedom of personal choice in matters of marriage and family life is one of the liberties protected by the Due Process Clause of the Fourteenth Amendment. . . . As we noted in Eisenstadt v Baird . . . there is a right "to be free from unwarranted governmental intrusion into matters so fundamentally affecting a person as the decision whether to bear or beget a child."

By acting to penalize the pregnant teacher for deciding to bear a child, overly restrictive maternity leave regulations can constitute a heavy burden on the exercise of these protected freedoms. Because public school maternity leave rules directly affect "one of the basic civil rights of man,". . .the Due Process Clause of the Fourteenth Amendment requires that such rules must not needlessly, arbitrarily, or capriciously impinge upon this vital area of a teacher's constitutional liberty. The question before us in these cases is whether the interests advanced in support of the rules of the Cleveland and Chesterfield County School Boards can justify the particular procedures they have adopted.

The school boards in these cases have offered two essentially overlapping explanations for their mandatory maternity leave rules. First, they contend that the firm cutoff dates are necessary to maintain continuity of classroom instruction, since advance knowledge of when a pregnant teacher must leave facilitates the finding and hiring of a qualified substitute. Secondly, the school boards seek to justify their maternity rules by arguing that at least some teachers become physically incapable of adequately performing certain of their duties during the latter part of pregnancy. By keeping the pregnant teacher out of the classroom during these final months, the maternity leave rules are said to protect the health of the teacher and her unborn child, while at the same time assuring that students have a physically capable instructor in the classroom at all times (footnote omitted).

It cannot be denied that continuity of instruction is a significant and legitimate educational goal. Regulations requiring pregnant teachers to provide early notice of their condition to school authorities undoubtedly facilitate administrative planning toward the important objective of continuity. But, as the Court of Appeals for the Second Circuit noted in Green v Waterford Board of Education. . .:

> "Where a pregnant teacher provides the Board with a date certain for commencement of leave. . .that value [continuity] is preserved; an arbitrary leave date set at the end of the fifth month is no more calculated to facilitate a planned and orderly transition between the teacher and a substitute than is a date fixed closer to confinement. Indeed, the latter. . .would afford the Board more, not less, time to procure a satisfactory long-term substitute." (Footnote omitted.)

Thus, while the advance-notice provisions in the Cleveland and Chesterfield County rules are wholly rational and may well be necessary to serve the objective of continuity of instruction, the absolute requirements of termination at the end of the fourth or fifth month of pregnancy are not. Were continuity the only goal, cutoff dates much later during pregnancy would serve as well as or better than the challenged rules, providing that ample advance notice requirements were retained. Indeed, continuity would seem just as well attained if the teacher herself were allowed to choose the date upon which to commence her leave, at least so long as the decision were required to be made and notice given of it well in advance of the date selected (foot-note omitted).

In fact, since the fifth or sixth month of pregnancy will obviously begin at different times in the school year for different teachers, the present Cleveland and Chesterfield County rules may serve to hinder attainment of the very continuity objectives that they are purportedly designed to promote. For example, the beginning of the fifth month of pregnancy for both Mrs. LaFleur and Mrs. Nelson occurred during March of 1971. Both were thus required to leave work with only a few months left in the school year, even though both were fully willing to serve through the end of the term (footnote omitted). Similarly, if con-tinuity were the only goal, it seems ironic that the Chesterfield County rule forced Mrs. Cohen to leave work in mid-December 1970 rather than at the end of the semester in January, as she requested.

We thus conclude that the arbitrary cutoff dates embodied in the mandatory leave rules before us have no rational relationship to the valid state interest of preserving continuity of instruction. As long as the teachers are required to give substantial advance notice of their condition, the choice of firm dates later in pregnancy would serve the boards' objectives just as well, while imposing a far lesser burden on the women's exercise of constitutionally protected freedom.

The question remains as to whether the cutoff dates at the begin-ning of the fifth and sixth months can be justified on the other ground advanced by the school boards—the necessity of keeping physically unfit teachers out of the classroom. There can be no doubt that such an objective is perfectly legitimate, both on educational and safety grounds. And, despite the plethora of conflicting medical testimony in these cases, we can assume, arguendo, that at least some teachers become physically disabled from effectively performing their duties during the latter stages of pregnancy.

The mandatory termination provisions of the Cleveland and Chesterfield County rules surely operate to insulate the classroom from the presence of potentially incapacitated pregnant teachers. But the question is whether the rules sweep too broadly . . . . That ques-tion must be answered in the affirmative, for the provisions amount to a conclusive presumption that every pregnant teacher who reaches the fifth or sixth month of pregnancy is physically incapable of continuing. There is no individualized determination by the teacher's doctor—or the school board's—as to any particular teacher's ability to continue at her job. The rules contain an irrebuttable presumption of physical incompetency, and that presumption applies even when the medical evidence as to an individual woman's physical status might be wholly to the contrary . . . .

. . . While the medical experts in these cases differed on many points, they unanimously agreed on one—the ability of any particular pregnant woman to continue at work past any fixed time in her pregnancy is very much an individual matter (footnote omitted). Even assuming, arguendo, that there are some women who would be physically unable to work past the particular cutoff dates embodied in the challenged rules, it is evident that there are large numbers of teachers who are fully capable of continuing work for longer than the Cleveland and Chesterfield County regulations will allow. Thus, the conclusive presumption embodied in these rules . . . is neither "necessarily [nor] universally true," and is violative of the Due Process Clause.

The school boards have argued that the mandatory termination dates serve the interest of administrative convenience, since there are many instances of teacher pregnancy, and the rules obviate the necessity for case-by-case determinations. Certainly, the boards have an interest in devising prompt and efficient procedures to achieve their legitimate objectives in this area. But, as the Court stated in Stanley v Illinois . . . :

> "[T]he Constitution recognizes higher values than speed and efficiency. Indeed, one might fairly say of the Bill of Rights in general, and the Due Process Clause in particular, that they were designed to protect the fragile values of a vulnerable citizenry from the overbearing concern for efficiency and efficacy that may characterize praiseworthy government officials no less, and perhaps more, than mediocre ones." (Footnote omitted.)

While it might be easier for the school boards to conclusively presume that all pregnant women are unfit to teach past the fourth or fifth month or even the first month, of pregnancy, administrative convenience alone is insufficient to make valid what otherwise is a violation of due process of law (footnote omitted). The Fourteenth Amendment requires the school boards to employ alternative administrative means, which do not so broadly infringe upon basic constitutional liberty, in support of their legitimate goals (footnote omitted).

We conclude, therefore, that neither the necessity for continuity of instruction nor the state interest in keeping physically unfit teachers out of the classroom can justify the sweeping mandatory leave regulations that the Cleveland and Chesterfield County School Boards have adopted. While the regulations no doubt represent a good-faith attempt to achieve a laudable goal, they cannot pass muster under the Due Process Clause of the Fourteenth Amendment, because they employ irrebuttable presumptions that unduly penalize a female teacher for deciding to bear a child.

III

In addition to the mandatory termination provisions, both the Cleveland and Chesterfield County rules contain limitations upon a teacher's eligibility to return to work after giving birth. Again, the school boards offer two justifications for the return rules—continuity of instruction and the desire to be certain that the teacher is physically competent when she returns to work. As is the case with the leave provisions, the question is not whether the school board's goals are legitimate, but rather whether the particular means chosen to achieve those objectives unduly infringe upon the teacher's constitutional liberty.

Under the Cleveland rule, the teacher is not eligible to return to work until the beginning of the next regular school semester following the time when her child attains the age of three months. A doctor's certificate attesting to the teacher's health is required before return; an additional physical examination may be required at the option of the school board.

The respondents. . . do not seriously challenge either the medical requirements of the Cleveland rule or the policy of limiting eligibility to return to the next semester following birth. The provisions concerning a medical certificate or supplemental physical examination are narrowly drawn methods of protecting the school board's interest in teacher fitness; these requirements allow an individualized decision as to the teacher's condition, and thus avoid the pitfalls of the presumptions inherent in the leave rules. Similarly, the provision limiting eligibility to return to the semester following delivery is a precisely drawn means of serving the school board's interest in avoiding unnecessary changes in classroom personnel during any one school term.

The Cleveland rule, however, does not simply contain these reasonable medical and next-semester eligibilty provisions. In addition, the school board requires the mother to wait until her child reaches the age of three months before the return rules begin to operate. The school board has offered no reasonable justification for this supplemental limitation, and we can perceive none. To the extent that the three-month provision reflects the school board's thinking that no mother is fit to return until that point in time, it suffers from the same constitutional deficiencies that plague the irrebuttable presumption in the termination rules (footnote omitted). The presumption, moreover, is patently unnecessary, since the requirement of a physician's certificate or a medical examination fully protects the school's interests in this regard. And finally, the three-month provision simply has nothing to do with continuity of instruction, since the precise point at which the child will reach the relevant age will obviously occur at a different point throughout the school year for each teacher.

Thus we conclude that the Cleveland return rule, insofar as it embodies the three-month age provision, is wholly arbitrary and irrational, and hence violates the Due Process Clause of the Fourteenth Amendment. The age limitation serves no legitimate state interest, and unnecessarily penalizes the female teacher for asserting her right to bear children.

We perceive no such constitutional infirmities in the Chesterfield County rule. In that school system, the teacher becomes eligible for re-employment upon submission of a medical certificate from her physician; return to work is guaranteed no later than the beginning of the next school year following the eligibility determination (footnote omitted). The medical certificate is both a reasonable and narrow method of protecting the school board's interest in teacher fitness, while the possible deferring of return until the next school year serves the goal of preserving continuity of instruction. In short, the Chesterfield County rule manages to serve the legitimate state interests here without employing unnecessary presumptions that broadly burden the exercise of protected constitutional liberty.

IV

For the reasons stated, we hold that the mandatory termination provisions of the Cleveland and Chesterfield County maternity regulations violate the Due Process Clause of the Fourteenth Amendment, because of their use of unwarranted conclusive presumptions that seriously burden the exercise of protected constitutional liberty. For similar reasons, we hold the three-month provision of the Cleveland return rule unconstitutional. . . .

Brooklyn Union Gas Co. v. State Human Rights Appeal Board, 41 N.Y.2d 84 (1976)

Jones, J. We hold that the provisions of subdivision 3 of section 205 of our State's Disability Benefits Law do not operate to shelter employment practices in the private sector that would otherwise be impermissibly discriminatory under our Human Rights Law. The imperative of the latter overrides the permissiveness of the former.

We have held that an employment personnel policy which singles out pregnancy and childbirth for treatment different from that accorded other instances of physical or medical impairment or disability is prohibited by the Human Rights Law . . . .

. . . Under the DBL, disability "caused by or arising in connection with a pregnancy" is excepted from the minimum benefits mandated by that law (§ 205, subd 3). We are urged to hold that the provisions of the DBL rather than those of the Human Rights Law (HRL) establish the minimum performance to be required of private employers—in effect that compliance with the minimum standards of the DBL will excuse failure to comply with the mandate of the HRL. We reject this conclusion.

There is an evident incongruity between the DBL and the HRL, and the determinative issue is which law shall be held to be operatively controlling. . . . The [DBL] fixed a floor, not a ceiling; it contained no prohibition against granting disability benefits in excess of those mandated by the DBL, thereby to supplement and to exceed the legislatively mandated minimum. . . .

In 1965 the Human Rights Law (Executive Law, art 15) was amended to prohibit discrimination in employment on account of sex. The new law laid down a blanket proscription applicable to all employers, public and private, with more than three employees (Executive Law, § 292, subd 5). . . . [T]he question is whether . . . the DBL now relieves private employers from the necessity of compliance with the mandate of the HRL. It does not have to be concluded that the HRL articulates a superior command, or that it reflects a worthier public policy than does the DBL; it suffices if it be recognized that the HRL expresses a *different* command. . . .

. . . We do not hold, then, that the HRL struck down the DBL; rather in areas within the reach of both statutes the HRL rendered the DBL dormant. In sum, the DBL and the HRL each lay down minimum demands on employers. Whichever statute imposes the greater obligation is the one which becomes operative. In the cases before us it is the HRL. . . .

APPENDIX B
Chapter 8 (Taxes)

Internal Revenue Code

SEC. 44A. Expenses for household and dependent care services necessary for gainful employment

(a) Allowances of credit.—In the case of an individual who maintains a household which includes as a member one or more qualifying individuals (as defined in subsection (c)(1)), there shall be allowed as a credit against the tax imposed by this chapter for the taxable year an amount equal to 20 percent of the employment-related expenses (as defined in subsection (c)(2)) paid by such individual during the taxable year.

(b) Application with other credits.—The credit allowed by subsection (a) shall not exceed the amount of the tax imposed by this chapter for the taxable year reduced by the sum of the credits allowable under—

(1) section 33 (relating to foreign tax credit),

(2) section 37 (relating to credit for the elderly),

(3) section 38 (relating to investment in certain depreciable property),

(4) section 40 (relating to expenses of work incentive programs),

(5) section 41 (relating to contributions to candidates for public office),

(6) section 42 (relating to general tax credit), and

(7) section 44 (relating to purchase of new principal residence).

(c) Definitions of qualifying individual and employment-related expenses.—For purposes of this section—

(1) **Qualifying individual.**—The term "qualifying individual" means—

(A) a dependent of the taxpayer who is under the age of 15 and with respect to whom the taxpayer is entitled to a deduction under section 151(e),

(B) a dependent of the taxpayer who is physically or mentally incapable of caring for himself, or

(C) the spouse of the taxpayer, if he is physically or mentally incapable of caring for himself.

(2) Employment-related expenses.—

(A) In General.—The term "employment-related expenses" means amounts paid for the following expenses, but only if such expenses are incurred to enable the taxpayer to be gainfully employed for any period for which there are one or more qualifying individuals with respect to the taxpayer:

(i) expenses for household services, and

(ii) expenses for the care of a qualifying individual.

(B) Exception.—Employment-related expenses described in subparagraph (A) which are incurred for services outside the taxpayer's household shall be taken into account only if incurred for the care of a qualifying individual described in paragraph (1)(A).

(d) Dollar limit on amount creditable.—The amount of the employment-related expenses incurred during any taxable year which may be taken into account under subsection (a) shall not exceed—

(1) $2,000 if there is one qualifying individual with respect to the taxpayer for such taxable year, or

(2) $4,000 if there are two or more qualifying individuals with respect to the taxpayer for such taxable year.

(e) Earned income limitation.—

(1) **In general.**—Except as otherwise provided in this subsection, the amount of the employment-related expenses incurred during any taxable year which may be taken into account under subsection (a) shall not exceed—

(A) in the case of an individual who is not married at the close of such year, such individual's earned income for such year, or

(B) in the case of an individual who is married at the close of such year, the lesser of such individual's earned income or the earned income of his spouse for such year.

(2) **Special rule for spouse who is a student or incapable of caring for himself.**—In the case of a spouse who is a student or a qualifying individual described in subsection (c)(1)(C), for purposes of paragraph (1), such spouse shall be deemed for each month during which such spouse is a full-time student at an educational institution, or is such a qualifying individual, to be gainfully employed and to have earned income of not less than—

(A) $166 if subsection (d)(1) applies for the taxable year, or

(B) $333 if subsection (d)(2) applies for the taxable year.

In the case of any husband and wife, this paragraph shall apply with respect to only one spouse for any one month.

(f) Special rules.—For purposes of this section—

(1) **Maintaining household.**—An individual shall be treated as maintaining a household for any period only if over half the cost of maintaining the household for such period is furnished by

such individual (or, if such individual is married during such period, is furnished by such individual and his spouse).

(2) **Married couples must file joint return.**—If the taxpayer is married at the close of the taxable year, the credit shall be allowed under subsection (a) only if the taxpayer and his spouse file a joint return for the taxable year.

(3) **Marital status.**—An individual legally separated from his spouse under a decree of divorce or of separate maintenance shall not be considered as married.

(4) **Certain married individuals living apart.**—If—

(A) an individual who is married and who files a separate return—

(i) maintains as his home a household which constitutes for more than one-half of the taxable year the principal place of abode of a qualifying individual, and

(ii) furnishes over half of the cost of maintaining such household during the taxable year, and

(B) during the last 6 months of such taxable year such individual's spouse is not a member of such household,

such individual shall not be considered as married.

(5) **Special dependency test in case of divorced parents, etc.**—If—

(A) a child (as defined in section 151(e)(3)) who is under the age of 15 or who is physically or mentally incapable of caring for himself receives over half of his support during the calendar year from his parents who are divorced or legally separated under a decree of divorce or separate maintenance or who are separated under a written separation agreement, and

(B) such child is in the custody of one or both of his parents for more than one-half of the calendar year,

in the case of any taxable year beginning in such calendar year such child shall be treated as being a qualifying individual described in subparagraph (A) or (B) of subsection (c)(1), as the case may be, with respect to that parent who has custody for a longer period during such calendar year than the other parent, and shall not be treated as being a qualifying individual with respect to such other parent.

(6) **Payments to related individuals.**—

(A) In general.—Except as provided in subparagraph (B), no credit shall be allowed under subsection (a) for any amount paid by the taxpayer to an individual bearing a relationship to the taxpayer described in paragraphs (1) through (8) of section 152(a) (relating to definition of dependent) or to a dependent described in paragraph (9) of such section.

(B) Exception.—Subparagraph (A) shall not apply to any amount paid by the taxpayer to an individual with respect to whom, for the taxable year of the taxpayer in which the service is performed, neither the taxpayer nor his spouse is entitled to a deduction under section 151(e) (relating to deduction for personal exemptions for dependents), but only if the service with respect to which such amount is paid constitutes employment within the meaning of section 3121(b).

(7) **Student.**—The term "student" means an individual who during each of 5 calendar months during the taxable year is a full-time student at an educational organization.

(8) **Educational organization.**—The term "educational organization" means an educational organization described in section 170(b)(1)(A)(ii).

(g) Regulations.—The Secretary shall prescribe such regulations as may be necessary to carry out the purposes of this section.

APPENDIX C
Chapter 10 (Insurance)

New York State Insurance Law, §§40-e, 162-a, 164-a.

§40-e. Discrimination because of sex or marital status
No association, corporation, firm, fund, individual, group, order, organization, society or trust shall refuse to issue any policy of insurance, or shall cancel or decline to renew such policy because of the sex or marital status of the applicant or policyholder.

§162-a. Maternity care coverage under group or blanket accident and health insurance policies
Every policy subject to the provisions of section one hundred sixty-two which provides hospital, surgical or medical coverage shall provide coverage for maternity care, including hospital, surgical or medical care to the same extent that hospital, surgical or medical coverage is provided for illness or disease under the policy, provided, however, that such maternity care coverage, other than coverage for complications of pregnancy, may be limited to reimbursement of covered expenses for maternity care for a period of four days of hospital confinement. Maternity care coverage may also be limited to those persons covered under the policy for a period of ten months, or for a lesser period if the pregnancy commenced while the insured was covered by the policy. The requirements of this section shall not be applicable, however, to any policies which have been or shall be issued to any "government" or "public employer," as those terms are defined in paragraph a of subdivision six of section two hundred one of the civil service law.

§164-a. Maternity care coverage under individual accident and sickness policies
Every policy subject to the provisions of section one hundred sixty-four which provides hospital, surgical or medical coverage shall provide coverage for maternity care, including hospital, surgical or medical care to the same extent that hospital, surgical or medical coverage is provided for illness or disease under the policy, provided, however, that such maternity care coverage, other than coverage for

complications of pregnancy, may be limited to reimbursement of covered expenses for maternity care for a period of four days of hospital confinement. Maternity care coverage may also be limited to those persons covered under the policy for a period of ten months, or for a lesser period if the pregnancy commenced while the insured was covered by the policy. The requirements of this section shall not be applicable, however, to any policies which have been or shall be issued to persons under a plan sponsored by any "government" or "public employer," as those terms are defined in paragraph a of subdivision six of section two hundred one of the civil service law, where such government or public employer pays all or part of the premium.

The above sections are applicable to all policies and contracts written, altered, amended or renewed after January 1, 1977.

APPENDIX D
Chapter 14 (Marriage and Divorce)

Morgan v. Morgan, 366 N.Y.S. 2d 978
(Sup. Ct. N.Y. Co., 1975)

Having determined the wife is entitled to a divorce, the basic issue now is:

Shall a young mother, presently a full-time pre-medical student with exceptional grades, be given an equal opportunity for development and fulfillment by completing her medical school training although capable of being self-supporting as a secretary? . . .

The parties were married on January 27, 1967 when the husband was in his third year pre-law course at the University of North Carolina and the wife, a sophomore, studying biology, at the Florida State University. Recognizing that both could not simultaneously continue their education and be self-supporting, they agreed that it would be preferable for him to finish his undergraduate and law school education while she worked. . . .

In the interim, Mrs. Morgan has become very proficient at shorthand and typing and also worked as a data analyst. I am satisfied that she is very skilled and, as an executive secretary or technician, could probably command an annual salary of at least $10,000 in normal economy and, very possibly, even in the present employment market.

In February 1973, she returned to the campus to pursue a full time educational career by undertaking a pre-medical course at Hunter College and her grades have been exceptional—a 3.83 general average (out of a 4.0 maximum) and an A score in the organic chemistry course, ranking 5th in a class of 70.

For his part, the husband has progressed well in his profession, having graduated from Columbia Law School after being selected for its Law Journal. His career started, as planned, with a one year stint as a law clerk to a Federal Circuit Judge and he immediately thereafter became an associate at a prominent Wall Street law firm. His . . . salary [is] $27,500. In all, he has done well and his future appears very promising. . . .

[One] consideration which bears upon my determination . . . is the total cost to both parties of hewing to the traditional approach of compelling the wife to spend her life working at a level far below her capabilities, both in terms of intellectual attainment, as well as from a monetary point of view.

. . . In this case, any possible short-term economic benefit which would result from the wife's returning to a position similar to the one she held over two years ago, is far outweighed by the potential benefit, economic, emotional and otherwise, of her pursuing her education.

In coming to the conclusion I do, I am seeking to effect a balancing of many factors—the parties' financial status, their obligations, age, station in life and opportunities for development and self-fulfillment. . . .

. . . Obviously two households cannot be maintained as cheaply as one and we therefore encounter the threshold issue of whether the wife—a very capable woman, probably able to earn at least $10,000 annually as a secretary or office worker—shall be compelled to contribute this sum, or a fair share thereof, to her own support, at this time, or shall she have an opportunity to achieve a professional education based upon her potential, which will be comparable to the one her husband received as a result of her assistance by working during their marriage.

In my opinion, the answer to this issue is that under these circumstances, the wife is also entitled to equal treatment and a "break" and should not be automatically relegated to a life of being a well-paid skilled technician laboring with a life-long frustration as to what her future might have been as a doctor, but for her marriage and motherhood.

I am impressed by the fact that the plaintiff does not assume the posture that she wants to be an alimony drone or seek permanent alimony. Rather she has indicated that she only wants support for herself until she finishes medical school in 5½ years (1½ years more in college and 4 years in medical school) and will try to work when possible.

In this regard, she merely seeks for herself the same opportunity which she helped give to the defendant.

Accordingly, I am directing that the defendant shall pay a total sum of $200 weekly for alimony and child support, so long as she does not remarry and continues to be a full-time student, undertaking a pre-medical or medical course.

APPENDIX E
Chapter 16 (Reproductive Freedom)

**Carey v. Population Services International,____U.S.____,
52 L. Ed 2d 675 (1977)**

Mr. Justice Brennan delivered the opinion of the Court (Parts I, II, III, and V), together with an opinion (Part IV), in which Mr. Justice Stewart, Mr. Justice Marshall, and Mr. Justice Blackmun joined.

Under New York Education Law §6811(8) it is a crime (1) for any person to sell or distribute any contraceptive of any kind to a minor under the age of 16 years; (2) for anyone other than a licensed pharmacist to distribute contraceptives to persons over 16; and (3) for anyone, including licensed pharmacists, to advertise or display contraceptives (footnote omitted). A three-judge District Court for the Southern District of New York declared §6811(8) unconstitutional in its entirety under the First and Fourteenth Amendments of the Federal Constitution insofar as it applies to nonprescription contraceptives, and enjoined its enforcement as so applied.... We affirm....

Although "[t]he Constitution does not explicitly mention any right of privacy," the Court has recognized that one aspect of the "liberty" protected by the Due Process Clause of the Fourteenth Amendment is "a right of personal privacy, or a guarantee of certain areas or zones of privacy."... This right of personal privacy includes "the interest in independence in making certain kinds of decisions."... While the outer limits of this aspect of privacy have not been marked by the Court, it is clear that among the decisions that an individual may make without unjustified government interference are personal decisions "relating to marriage,... procreation,... contraception,... family relationships,... and child rearing and education....

The decision whether or not to beget or bear a child is at the very heart of this cluster of constitutionally protected choices. That decision holds a particularly important place in the history of the right of privacy, a right first explicitly recognized in an opinion holding unconstitutional a statute prohibiting the use of contraceptives... and most prominently vindicated in recent years in the contexts of contraception . . . and abortion. . . . This is understandable, for in a field that by definition concerns the most intimate of human activities and relationships, decisions whether to accomplish or to prevent conception are among the most private and sensitive. "If the right of privacy means anything, it is the right of the individual, married or single, to be free of unwarranted governmental intrusion into matters so fundamentally affecting a person as the decision whether to bear or beget a child." . . .

That the constitutionally protected right of privacy extends to an individual's liberty to make choices regarding contraception does not, however, automatically invalidate every state regulation in this area. The business of manufacturing and selling contraceptives may be regulated in ways that do not infringe protected individual choices. And even a burdensome regulation may be validated by a sufficiently compelling state interest. In Roe v Wade, for example, after determining that the "right of privacy . . . encompass[es] a woman's decision whether or not to terminate her pregnancy," . . . we cautioned that the right is not absolute, and that certain state interests (in that case, "interests in safeguarding health, in maintaining medical standards, and in protecting potential life") may at some point "become sufficiently compelling to sustain regulation of the factors that govern the abortion decision." . . . "Compelling" is of course the key word; where a decision as fundamental as that whether to bear or beget a child is involved, regulations imposing a burden on it may be justified only by compelling state interests, and must be narrowly drawn to express only those interests . . . .

The District Court . . . held unconstitutional, as applied to nonprescription contraceptives, the provision . . . prohibiting the distribution of contraceptives to those under 16 years of age (footnote omitted). Appellants contend that this provision of the statute is constitutionally permissible as a regulation of the morality of minors, in furtherance of the State's policy against promiscuous sexual intercourse among the young.

The question of the extent of state power to regulate conduct of minors not constitutionally regulable when committed by adults is a vexing one, perhaps not susceptible to precise answer. We have been reluctant to attempt to define "the totality of the relationship of the juvenile and the state." . . . Certain principles, however, have been recognized. "Minors, as well as adults, are protected by the Constitution and possess constitutional rights." . . . "[W]hatever may be their precise impact, neither the Fourteenth Amendment nor the Bill of Rights is for adults alone." . . . On the other hand, we have held in a variety of contexts that "the power of the state to control the conduct of children reaches beyond the scope of its authority over adults." . . .

Of particular significance to the decision of this case, the right to privacy in connection with decisions affecting procreation extends to minors as well as to adults. Planned Parenthood of Central Missouri v Danforth, supra, held that a State "may not impose a blanket provision . . . requiring the consent of a parent or person in loco parentis as a condition for abortion of an unmarried minor during the first 12 weeks of her pregnancy." . . .

Since the State may not impose a blanket prohibition, or even a blanket requirement of parental consent, on the choice of a minor to terminate her pregnancy, the constitutionality of a blanket prohibition of the distribution of contraceptives to minors is a fortiori foreclosed. The State's interests in protection of the mental and physical health of the pregnant minor, and in protection of potential life are clearly more implicated by the abortion decision than by the decision to use a non-hazardous contraceptive.

Appellants argue, however, that significant state interests are served by restricting minors' access to contraceptives, because free availability to minors of contraceptives would lead to increased sexual activity among the young, in violation of the policy of New York to discourage such behavior (footnote omitted). The argument is that minors' sexual activity may be deterred by increasing the hazards attendant on it. The same argument, however, would support a ban on abortions for minors, or indeed support a prohibition on abortions, or access to contraceptives, for the unmarried, whose sexual activity is also against the public policy of many States. Yet, in each of these areas, the Court has rejected the argument, noting in Roe v Wade, that "no court of commentator has taken the argument seriously." . . . The reason for this unanimous rejection was stated in Eisenstadt v Baird, supra: "It would be plainly unreasonable to assume that [the state] has prescribed pregnancy and the birth of an unwanted child [or the physical and psychological dangers of an abortion] as punishment for fornication." . . . We remain reluctant to attribute any such "scheme of values" to the State (footnote omitted). . . .

Affirmed.

Roe v. Wade, 410 U.S. 113 (1973)

Mr. Justice Blackmun delivered the opinion of the Court:
. . . The Constitution does not explicitly mention any right of privacy. In a line of decisions, however, going back perhaps as far as [1891], the Court has recognized that a right of personal privacy, or a guarantee of certain areas or zones of privacy, does exist under the Constitution. In varying contexts, the Court or individual Justices have, indeed, found at least the roots of that right in the First Amendment. . . . These decisions make it clear that only personal rights that can be deemed "fundamental" or "implicit in the concept of ordered

liberty," are included in this guarantee of personal privacy. They also make it clear that the right has some extension to activities relating to marriage. . . .

This right of privacy . . . is broad enough to encompass a woman's decision whether or not to terminate her pregnancy. The detriment that the State would impose upon the pregnant woman by denying this choice altogether is apparent. Specific and direct harm medically diagnosable even in early pregnancy may be involved. Maternity, or additional offspring, may force upon the woman a distressful life and future. Psychological harm may be imminent. Mental and physical health may be taxed by child care. There is also the distress, for all concerned, associated with the unwanted child, and there is the problem of bringing a child into a family already unable, psychologically and otherwise, to care for it. In other cases, as in this one, the additional difficulties and continuing stigma of unwed motherhood may be involved. All these are factors the woman and her responsible physician necessarily will consider in consultation.

On the basis of elements such as these, appellant and some amici argue that the woman's right is absolute and that she is entitled to terminate her pregnancy at whatever time, in whatever way, and for whatever reason she alone chooses. With this we do not agree. . . .

The Court's decisions recognizing a right of privacy also acknowledge that some state regulation in areas protected by the right is appropriate. As noted above, a State may properly assert important interests in safeguarding health, in maintaining medical standards, and in protecting potential life. At some point in pregnancy, these respective interests become sufficiently compelling to sustain regulation of the factors that govern the abortion decision. The privacy right involved, therefore, cannot be said to be absolute. . . .

We, therefore, conclude that the right of personal privacy includes the abortion decision, but that this right is not unqualified and must be considered against important state interests in regulation. . . .

Where certain "fundamental rights" are involved, the Court has held that regulation limiting these rights may be justified only by a "compelling state interest," . . . and that legislative enactments must be narrowly drawn to express only the legitimate state interests at stake. . . .

The District Court held that the appellee failed to meet his burden of demonstrating that the Texas statute's infringement upon Roe's rights was necessary to support a compelling state interest, and that, although the appellee presented "several compelling justifications for state presence in the area of abortions," the statutes outstripped these justifications and swept "far beyond any areas of compelling state interest." . . . Appellant and appellee both contest that holding. Appellant, as has been indicated, claims an absolute right that bars any state imposition of criminal penalties in the area. Appellee argues that the State's determination to recognize and protect prenatal life from and after conception constitutes a compelling state interest. As noted above, we do not agree fully with either formulation.

The appellee and certain amici argue that the fetus is a "person" within the language and meaning of the Fourteenth Amendment. In support of this, they outline at length and in detail the well-known facts of fetal development. If this suggestion of personhood is established, the appellant's case, of course, collapses...for the fetus' right to life is then guaranteed specifically by the Amendment. The appellant conceded as much on reargument. On the other hand, the appellee conceded on reargument that no case could be cited that holds that a fetus is a person within the meaning of the Fourteenth Amendment.

...But in nearly all...instances [in which the word "person" is used in the Constitution] the use of the word is such that it has application only postnatally. None indicates, with any assurance, that it has any possible prenatal application.

All this, together with our observation...that throughout the major portion of the 19th century prevailing legal abortion practices were far freer than they are today, persuades us that the word "person," as used in the Fourteenth Amendment, does not include the unborn....

This conclusion, however, does not of itself fully answer the contentions raised by Texas, and we pass on to other considerations.

The pregnant woman cannot be isolated in her privacy. She carries an embryo and, later, a fetus, if one accepts the medical definitions of the developing young in the human uterus....The situation therefore is inherently different from marital intimacy, or bedroom possession of obscene material, or marriage, or procreation, or education....As we have intimated above, it is reasonable and appropriate for a State to decide that at some point in time another interest, that of health of the mother or that of potential human life, becomes significantly involved. The woman's privacy is no longer sole and any right of privacy she possesses must be measured accordingly.

Texas urges that, apart from the Fourteenth Amendment, life begins at conception and is present throughout pregnancy, and that, therefore, the State has a compelling interest in protecting that life from and after conception. We need not resolve the difficult question of when life begins. When those trained in the respective disciplines of medicine, philosophy, and theology are unable to arrive at any consensus, the judiciary, at this point in the development of man's knowledge, is not in a position to speculate as to the answer.

It should be sufficient to note briefly the wide divergence of thinking on this most sensitive and difficult question. There has always been strong support for the view that life does not begin until live birth....

In areas other than criminal abortion, the law has been reluctant to endorse any theory that life, as we recognize it, begins before live birth or to accord legal rights to the unborn except in narrowly defined situations and except when the rights are contingent upon live birth. . . . In short, the unborn have never been recognized in the law as persons in the whole sense.

In view of all this, we do not agree that, by adopting one theory of life, Texas may override the rights of the pregnant woman that are at stake. We repeat, however, that the State does have an important and legitimate interest in preserving and protecting the health of the pregnant woman. . . and that it has still *another* important and legitimate interest in protecting the potentiality of human life. These interests are separate and distinct. Each grows in substantiality as the woman approaches term and, at a point during pregnancy, each becomes "compelling."

With respect to the State's important and legitimate interest in the health of the mother, the "compelling" point, in the light of present medical knowledge, is at approximately the end of the first trimester. This is so because of the now-established medical fact, . . . that until the end of the first trimester mortality in abortion may be less than mortality in normal childbirth. It follows that, from and after this point, a State may regulate the abortion procedure to the extent that the regulation reasonably relates to the preservation and protection of maternal health. Examples of permissible state regulation in this area are requirements as to the qualifications of the person who is to perform the abortion; as to the facility in which the procedure is to be performed, that is, whether it must be a hospital or may be a clinic or some other place of less-than-hospital status; as to the licensing of the facility; and the like.

This means, on the other hand, that, for the period of pregnancy prior to this "compelling" point, the attending physician, in consultation with his patient, is free to determine, without regulation by the State, that, in his medical judgment, the patient's pregnancy should be terminated. If that decision is reached, the judgment may be effectuated by an abortion free of interference by the State.

With respect to the State's important and legitimate interest in potential life, the "compelling" point is at viability. This is so because the fetus then presumably has the capability of meaningful life outside the mother's womb. State regulation protective of fetal life after viability thus has both logical and biological justifications. If the State is interested in protecting fetal life after viability, it may go so far as to proscribe abortion during that period, except when it is necessary to preserve the life or health of the mother.

Measured against these standards, the Texas Penal Code, in restricting legal abortions to those "procured or attempted by medical advice for the purpose of saving the life of the mother," sweeps too broadly. The statute makes no distinction between abortions performed early in pregnancy and those performed later, and it limits to a single reason, "saving" the mother's life, the legal justification for the procedure. The statute, therefore, cannot survive the constitutional attack made upon it here.

Planned Parenthood of Central Missouri v. Danforth
428 U.S. 788 (1976)

Section 3(3) [of the statute] requires the prior written consent of the spouse of the woman seeking an abortion during the first 12 weeks of pregnancy, unless "the abortion is certified by a licensed physician to be necessary in order to preserve the life of the mother." . . .

In *Roe* and *Doe* we specifically reserved decision on the question whether a requirement for consent by the father of the fetus, by the spouse, or by the parents, or a parent, of an unmarried minor, may be constitutionally imposed. We now hold that the State may not constitutionally require the consent of the spouse, as a condition for abortion during the first 12 weeks of pregnancy. . . . Clearly, since the State cannot regulate or proscribe abortion during the first stage, [of pregnancy] when the physician and his patient make that decision, the State cannot delegate authority to any particular person, even the spouse, to prevent abortion during that same period.

We are not unaware of the deep and proper concern and interest that a devoted and protective husband has in his wife's pregnancy and in the growth and development of the fetus she is carrying. Neither has this Court failed to appreciate the importance of the marital relationship in our society. Moreover, we recognize that the decision whether to undergo or to forgo an abortion may have profound effects on the future of any marriage, effects that are both physical and mental, and possibly deleterious. Notwithstanding these factors, we cannot hold that the State has the constitutional authority to give the spouse unilaterally the ability to prohibit the wife from terminating her pregnancy, when the State itself lacks that right.

It seems manifest that, ideally, the decision to terminate a pregnancy should be one concurred in by both the wife and her husband. No marriage may be viewed as harmonious or successful if the marriage partners are fundamentally divided on so important and vital an issue. But it is difficult to believe that the goal of fostering mutuality and trust in a marriage, and of strengthening the marital relationship and the marriage institution, will be achieved by giving the husband a veto power exercisable for any reason whatsoever or for no reason at all. Even if the State had the ability to delegate to the husband a power it itself could not exercise, it is not at all likely that such action would further, as the District Court majority phrased it, the "interest of the state in protecting the mutuality of decisions vital to the marriage relationship."

We recognize, of course, that when a woman, with the approval of her physician but without the approval of her husband, decides to terminate her pregnancy, it could be said that she is acting unilaterally.

The obvious fact is that when the wife and the husband disagree on this decision, the view of only one of the two marriage partners can prevail. Since it is the woman who physically bears the child and who is the more directly and immediately affected by the pregnancy, as between the two, the balance weighs in her favor....

Section 3(4) [of the statute] requires, with respect to the first 12 weeks of pregnancy, where the woman is unmarried and under the age of 18 years, the written consent of a parent or person *in loco parentis* unless, again, "the abortion is certified by a licensed physician as necessary in order to preserve the life of the mother." It is to be observed that only one parent need consent....

We agree with appellants...that the State may not impose a blanket provision..., requiring the consent of a parent or person *in loco parentis* as a condition for abortion of an unmarried minor during the first 12 weeks of her pregnancy. Just as with the requirement of consent from the spouse, so here, the State does not have the constitutional authority to give a third party an absolute, and possibly arbitrary, veto over the decision of the physician and his patient to terminate the patient's pregnancy, regardless of the reason for withholding the consent.

Constitutional rights do not mature and come into being magically only when one attains the state-defined age of majority. Minors, as well as adults, are protected by the Constitution and possess constitutional rights. The Court indeed, however, long has recognized that the State has somewhat broader authority to regulate the activities of children than of adults.

It remains, then, to examine whether there is any significant state interest in conditioning an abortion on the consent of a parent or person *in loco parentis* that is not present in the case of an adult.

One suggested interest is the safeguarding of the family unit and of parental authority. It is difficult, however, to conclude that providing a parent with absolute power to overrule a determination, made by the physician and his minor patient, to terminate the patient's pregnancy will serve to strengthen the family unit. Neither is it likely that such veto power will enhance parental authority or control where the minor and the nonconsenting parent are so fundamentally in conflict and the very existence of the pregnancy already has fractured the family structure. Any independent interest the parent may have in the termination of the minor daughter's pregnancy is no more weighty than the right of privacy of the competent minor mature enough to have become pregnant.

Eve Cary was, for the last seven years, a staff attorney at the New York Civil Liberties Union, where she specialized in women's rights law. She has recently begun work at the Criminal Appeals Bureau of the Legal Aid Society in New York City. She has written two previous books, *The Rights of Students* and *Woman and the Law.*